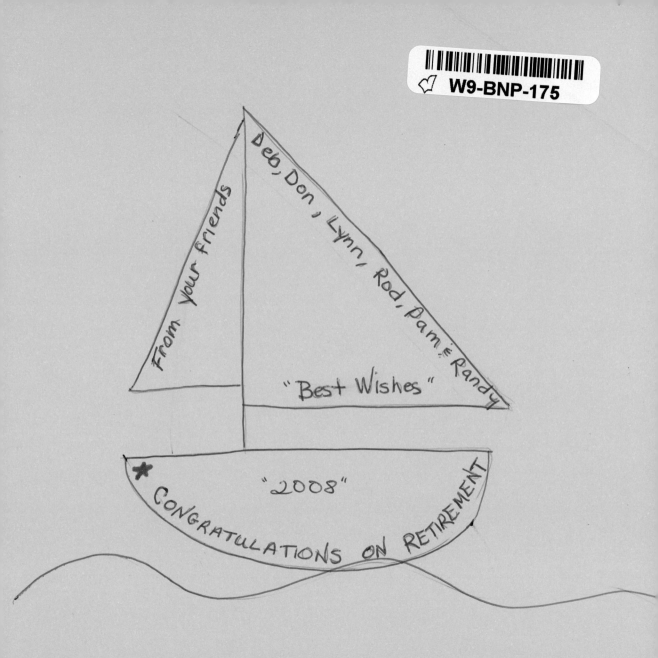

FIFTY PLACES TO SAIL

BEFORE YOU DIE

FIFTY PLACES TO
SAIL
BEFORE YOU DIE

Sailing Experts Share
the World's Greatest Destinations

✳

Chris Santella

STEWART, TABORI & CHANG

NEW YORK

To Deidre, Cassidy Rose, and Annabel Blossom,
who've been unwaveringly patient and generous with their time
so I might pursue my dream of writing books.

✳

ALSO BY THE AUTHOR

Fifty Places to Fly Fish Before You Die:
Fly-Fishing Experts Share the World's Greatest Destinations

Fifty Places to Golf Before You Die:
Golf Experts Share the World's Greatest Destinations

Fifty Favorite Fly-Fishing Tales:
Expert Fly Anglers Share Stories from the Sea and Stream

Contents

ACKNOWLEDGMENTS

This book would not have been possible without the generous assistance of the expert sailors who shared their time and experiences to help bring these fifty great sailing venues to life. To these men and women, I offer the most heartfelt thanks. I would especially like to thank Sue Maffei Plowden (Suma, to her friends), who offered much advice and countless introductions to her vast circle of sailing pals. I also want to acknowledge the fine efforts of my editors Jennifer Levesque, Dervla Kelly, and Kate Norment, designer Paul Wagner, and copyeditors Sylvia Karchmar and Elizabeth Norment, who helped bring the book into being despite a deadline baby (Jennifer's first, Veronica Rose) and a very late manuscript delivery. These folks do a wonderful job; as I'm fond of saying, if the words are half as good as the aesthetics of the book itself, it won't be a terrible read! Thanks should also go to my agent Stephanie Kip Rostan, who talked me off the ledge on more than one occasion (due to said late manuscript delivery). Last, I'd like to thank my parents, who didn't insist that I take sailing lessons, but encouraged me to try new things and constantly expand my horizons . . . and my wife, Deidre, and daughters, Cassidy Rose and Annabel Blossom, who have shown such tremendous love, patience, and support as I wrestle against deadline after deadline.

FOREWORD

Water occupies over 70 percent of the planet Earth, providing a multitude of sailing venues, from high-latitude exploration to sultry equatorial islands and all of the seas, bays, and lakes in between. To some offshore sailors these waterways provide "highways" to travel from place to place; to racing sailors they are a unique playing field that is ever changing with the weather; to cruising sailors they provide a peaceful setting to while away time—and for all, being at sea is a welcome break from life ashore.

Working in the sailing industry around the world has provided me with a lifetime of opportunities to make friends who share a common bond of spending time on the water. Often we return to the same places—a favorite regatta in Newport or Sardinia, a familiar anchorage in Maine or New Zealand—while other times an invitation to try something new takes us farther afield—to Turkey, Antarctica, or the fjords of Alaska.

In *Fifty Places to Sail Before You Die*, Chris Santella has interviewed professional sailors, writers, boatbuilders, former Olympians, sailing instructors, yachting photographers, and others to find out their favorite places, and has endeavored to bring these places to life. Some of these you may know, but the description of others is likely to spur you on to pack your duffle and head out to explore some intriguing destinations.

In ports and harbors around the world there are always people to be found doing just what we all like to do: mess around in boats in a special place. I hope this title helps lead you to new ports and new friends.

—SUSAN MAFFEI PLOWDEN

INTRODUCTION

I will be the first to admit that my sailing experience is somewhat limited: a season's worth of sailing lessons at Boothbay Harbor Yacht Club in the summer of 1975, with a cruel crewmate who yelled "Shark!" each time we tacked (this, take note, was the year that *Jaws* was released); and several corporate events that transpired on sailboats in the San Francisco Bay where I was compelled to discuss the benefits of various technologies that I didn't fully understand (as the marketing guy, I was not required to understand much of anything). Despite these rather unpromising forays into the sport, I must say that several key facets of sailing—a chance to be outside on the water in the company of friends, perhaps in the spirit of gentlemanly competition—have always been appealing. When the opportunity to write *Fifty Places to Sail Before You Die* arose, I saw it as a chance to explore this passion that grips millions of men and women around the world.

To expand my horizons—and to get a real aficionado's sense of what the sailing experience offers—I followed a recipe that served me well in my first two Fifty Places books: seeking the advice of some professionals. I interviewed a host of people closely connected with the sport to learn about some of their favorite waters and sailing experiences. These experts range from professional sailors (like Gary Jobson and Mike Sanderson) to boat builders (like Jeff Johnstone) to Olympians (like J. J. Isler) to journalists and photographers (like Herb McCormick and Billy Black) to instructors (like Penny Whiting) to educators (like Peter Mello) to adventurers (like Skip Novak and Lin and Larry Pardey). Some spoke of waters that are near and dear to their hearts, others spoke of places they've only visited once but that made a profound impression. People appreciate sailing for many different reasons, and this range of attractions is evidenced here. (To give a sense of the breadth of their sailing backgrounds, a biography of each individual is included after each essay.)

While this book comprises fifty great sailing experiences, it by no means attempts to rank the places discussed, or the quality of the experience each body of water affords. Such ranking is largely subjective; the venue that might be appealing to a serious racer could very well be anathema to a weekend cruiser. In this spirit, the places are listed alphabetically by state or country.

OPPOSITE
On the Sea of Cortez, cruisers enjoy calm waters and a reliable afternoon breeze.

In the hope that a few readers might embark on adventures of their own, I have provided some brief "If You Go" information at the end of each chapter. It is by no means exhaustive, and no attempt has been made to address the many concerns an international cruiser needs to consider (that is well beyond the scope of this project). However, it's hoped that these notes will give would-be travelers a starting point for planning their trip. This information includes basic "getting there" options for those who might be traveling by air and chartering a boat; the best time to visit, based on climate and nautical goings-on; charter options for bareboaters (or skippered cruises if no bareboat options are available—for example, few would endeavor to go it on their own to South Georgia Island or Spitsbergen); mooring options for those areas where mooring might require more than merely dropping anchor; and on-shore accommodations.

From the relative indolence of cruising the Dodecanese or the British Virgin Islands, to the white-knuckle adventure of rounding Cape Horn, to the thrill of partaking in a regatta off Newport, *Fifty Places to Sail Before You Die* attempts to capture the rich and varied world of recreational sailing. It's my hope that it will inspire you to set sail on some new adventures of your own.

OPPOSITE
Biscayne Bay
offers first-rate
racing and
equally good
cruising.

The Destinations

Alaska

RESURRECTION BAY

RECOMMENDED BY **Deborah Altermatt**

During the Alaskan gold rush at the turn of the last century, most fortune-seekers arrived via sailboat and quickly took to the interior. Some who arrive in the forty-ninth state today stay closer to the coast—and as Deborah Altermatt relates, that may be a more rewarding decision.

"We came to Seward in 1994 and it wasn't long before we sailed in Resurrection Bay," Deborah recalled. "Soon after, we purchased a sailboat. It's really the best way to explore the region. To reach many places, it's the only way."

It would be an understatement to say that Alaska has a great deal of shoreline to explore: 47,300 miles unfold, from the northernmost reaches on the Beaufort Sea near Barrow to the southeast region that snakes along the northwestern edge of British Columbia. This staggering amount of terrain amounts to more shoreline than that of the lower forty-eight states combined! The relatively finite stretch from Seward to Sitka—a mere 500 miles from north to south, with just 15,000 miles of shoreline—sees the great majority of Alaska's recreational maritime traffic, much of this in the form of cruise ships plying the famed "Inside Passage." Cruise-ship passengers get to take in some marvelous sights—Glacier Bay, for example—and have opportunities to purchase T-shirts and other assorted trinkets in each port of call. However, they miss the chance to tuck into more isolated fjords where one can get up close and personal with glaciers, sea lions, and other facets of the Alaska landscape.

Many voyagers use Seward and Resurrection Bay as a point of departure for Inside Passage adventures. Deborah sees little reason to venture afield from her home waters. "The sailing conditions in Resurrection Bay are pretty darn ideal," she explained. "The wind blows 15 to 20 knots most of the time. It comes from the north in the a.m., when

OPPOSITE
Alaskan sailors can get up close and personal with massive glaciers.

you're most likely to be sailing south; in the afternoon, it comes off the Gulf of Alaska, from the south, when you're likely to be heading back to Seward. The water is generally 100 fathoms deep, so there are few hazards to deal with, and there are countless sheltered anchoring spots. If you sail south from Seward and hang a left, you're in Prince William Sound. If you hang a right, you're in Kenai Fjords National Park."

It's the fjords and glaciers—the dramatic counterpoint of the sea and cliffs of basalt and ice—that make the shoreline of the Alaska panhandle so enchanting to behold. That, and the many animals that call the waters and the thin strips of forest among the ice fields home. Viewing an 8,000-foot peak when you're standing at an altitude of 5,000 feet is impressive; seeing that same elevation gain from sea level can take your breath away. "Most cruising visitors take in the glaciers and other fjord attractions farther south," Deborah added. "You can see all the same things in Kenai Fjords National Park, but without the crowds."

Kenai Fjords National Park encompasses over 600,000 acres on the southeast coast of the Kenai Peninsula, and includes two significant ice fields—Harding and Grewingk-Yalik—which are occasionally punctuated by mountains from the Kenai Range. The ice fields have had a significant effect in forging the jutted, rutted landscape. The ice fields slowly melt, giving birth to glaciers, which can be thought of as rivers of ice. As the glaciers recede, they slowly carve away canyons of rock, which are filled in by seawater to create fjords. Eight tidewater glaciers stretch down to the ocean surface in the borders of the park. When such a glacier "calves" (sheds portions of ice) to create small icebergs, the roar of shearing ice echoes through the fjords and can be heard miles away; waves large enough to upset a small craft are sometimes generated by the impact of ice and water.

The animal life of coastal Alaska is as much an attraction for seafarers as the awe-inspiring scenery. In and around the fjords of Resurrection Bay, you may encounter Steller sea lions, Dall porpoises, gray, humpback, minke and killer whales (orcas), and countless sea birds, including common murres and horned and tufted puffins; you'll definitely come upon sea otters, which are extremely abundant (and, in Deborah's opinion, incredibly cute). The region's more landlocked inhabitants—moose, mountain goats, and the occasional black or brown bear—can sometimes be viewed from the water. Bald eagles are a dime a dozen in this part of the world; after you've been in Alaska a few days, you'll barely look up as one of these majestic birds flies overhead.

When asked to name a favorite itinerary, Deborah suggested a quick cruise to a spot called Thumb Cove. "It's just seven miles or so from Seward. During the off-season when we're not running tours or charters, we can take off after work and be there by seven p.m. Even in late April, it's light until eleven, so there's plenty of time to set up and/or explore. You anchor in an amphitheater of tall mountains that have glaciers. Often we'll see foraging bears and mountain goats from the boat. Pods of orcas will sometimes come into the cove and 'sing' to us. Once we've anchored, we'll dinghy to the beach. Some people will camp there; others may get a cabin [provided for a nominal fee by the Forest Service] nearby. We'll make a great driftwood bonfire. Next morning we'll have mimosas on the deck of the boat, while eagles soar above us. We'll pull anchor by lunchtime, and if all goes right, we'll have the southerly breeze to push us home."

Deborah Altermatt came to Alaska in 1977 with her husband to teach school in the Alaskan bush. She learned to sail on a small lake in the interior after being inspired by regattas she witnessed during a vacation on the French Riviera. She came to Seward in 1994 and took a sailing class from Sailing, Inc. (www.sailinginc.com); a few months later, she bought the business, which she continues to operate today, offering day sails, sailing instruction, and yacht brokering. Deborah offers would-be sailors some sage counsel: "When you buy a sailboat, watch out. You never know how it will change your life!"

IF YOU GO

➤ **Getting There:** Most visitors reach Seward by flying into Anchorage and either renting a car, or taking a motorcoach or a train south. Motorcoach and rail options are described in detail at Alaska Tour & Travel (800-208-0200; www.alaskatravel.com).

➤ **Best Time to Visit:** May through August will provide the most temperate weather.

➤ **Charter Operators:** Sailing, Inc. (907-224-3160; www.sailinginc.com) provides bareboat charters on a limited basis. Skippered charter providers include Alaskan Sailing Charters (866-486-1732; www.kodiaksailingcharters.com).

➤ **Moorings:** Moorings are available in the Seward Small Boat Harbor (907-224-3138; www.cityofseward.net/harbor).

➤ **On-Shore Accommodations:** The Seward Visitors & Convention Bureau (907-224-8051; www.sewardak.org) outlines lodgings options.

ANTARCTIC PENINSULA

RECOMMENDED BY **Gary Jobson**

Some wags may joke about professional sailors always heading off to "all ends of the earth." Gary Jobson has taken the phrase quite literally, embarking on not one but several trips to Antarctica.

"My inspiration to go south to explore Antarctica came from covering the America's Cup in San Diego in 1993," Gary began. "There wasn't much wind that year, and frankly, I thought the racing was a bit boring. After this experience, I thought it would be interesting to build a TV episode around a trip to a place that was *windy*. Cape Horn immediately came to mind. When I suggested this to the producers, someone suggested that we do something even wilder. And what's wilder than Cape Horn? Antarctica! I made my first trip there in 1993, and returned again in 1996."

Antarctica is not one of the world's most welcoming places. This is evidenced by the fact that there are no indigenous people on the continent, despite the fact that Antarctica encompasses over 14 million square miles, roughly one and a half times the size of the United States! (A contingent of 5,000 scientists from the twenty-seven nations that are signatories of the Antarctic Treaty maintain a year-round presence on the continent; another 25,000 or so tourists visit each season.) A great majority of the landmass—an estimated 98 percent—consists of ice and snow that has an average thickness of 7,000 feet; scientists believe that up to 70 percent of the world's fresh water is contained here. ("If the ice stored in Antarctica were to melt," Gary observed, "the world's oceans would rise 200 feet.") While precipitation can reach the equivalent of 36 inches of water on the Antarctic Peninsula, the continent's wettest region, only an inch of precipitation reaches the South Pole. During the winter months, when temperatures hover in the balmy range of -40 to -90 degrees Fahrenheit, seawater surrounding the continent freezes up to 200

OPPOSITE
The window
for sailing to
Antarctica is
in the southern-
hemisphere
summer—from
December to
March.

miles offshore, covering an area even larger than Antarctica's landmass. In the summer (December through March), the freeze recedes, and a brief window opens for sailing to the more northerly portions of Antarctica.

Given its location and inhospitable terrain, it's not surprising that the Antarctic continent went undiscovered until fairly recent times. Captain James Cook, in his relentless search for the "southern continent," crossed the Antarctic Circle in 1773 and again in 1774, though ice prevented him from ever reaching the landmass itself. (He did, however, come upon New Zealand and Tahiti on this voyage.) Sealers and whalers worked the icy waters around Antarctica in the early 1800s, and subsequent national expeditions sponsored by Britain and Russia confirmed that the landmass was indeed a continent and not merely a collection of islands. Over the next hundred years, many expeditions were led to Antarctica. One of the most scientifically productive was the "Belgica" expedition, conducted by the Geographical Royal Society from Brussels in 1898–99; certainly the most famous was Sir Ernest Shackleton's 1914 attempt to cross the Antarctic continent on foot. (Despite having their ship, *Endurance*, crushed by pack ice some 80 miles offshore, Shackleton and his crew emerged after a twenty-month ordeal—including an 800-mile crossing in an open boat—with no loss of life.)

Gary Jobson's voyages to Antarctica were a bit less perilous than Sir Ernest's, yet for most they would still qualify as high adventure. "It's one thing to go down there in a large cruise ship; it's quite another to go in a 54-foot sailboat," Gary continued. "I believe that when you see things by sailboat, you really have a chance to connect with your environment. If you're traveling at 6 or 8 knots, you're moving slowly enough to take in everything. You really get the feel of what the ice floes are all about. Icebergs are impressive when they're a half-mile away. They're really something when you're next to them, fifty feet away. It's shocking how loud these dynamic entities are. They're cracking, rolling over, there are chunks falling off. At one point we were about a quarter mile away from an iceberg that was the size of a stadium, and we were about to cruise closer to get a better look when the whole thing rolled, sending a big wave in our direction. After that, we kept our distance."

There are two things you can depend on when cruising around Antarctica: a degree of foul weather, and encounters with marine wildlife. Skip Novak, a sailor who leads expeditions to the area, estimates that upon arrival, roughly 50 percent of the time in Antarctica is spent stormbound in anchorage. "On one of our trips, we got holed up in this little cove;

it was so rough and so cold that we couldn't proceed," Gary recalled. "We were stuck there for nine days. We had nine people on board, and we certainly got on each other's nerves. To make matters worse, we all came down with the flu."

If Antarctica is lacking in warmth, it is certainly rich in krill, a tiny shrimplike crustacean that is the foundation of the region's food chain. "If you totaled the biomass of krill around Antarctica, it would be greater than the biomass of all the humans in the world," Gary ventured. The krill provides food for penguins, seals, and whales; the penguins and seals in turn become prey for leopard seals and killer whales. "The penguins are more athletic than you'd think," Gary said. "They have to be quite powerful to jump out of the water onto the ice as they do. One thing that *National Geographic* and *March of the Penguins* don't tell you is just how putrid a colony of penguins smells!"

Leopard seals, which frequent pack ice during the more clement months, are predators unique to the region, and the only seals that will devour other seals. They're easily identified by their slightly reptilian head, and a white throat that's decorated with black spots. "Leopard seals have this crooked smile, which adds to their sinister reputation," Gary observed. "You don't want to find yourself out on the ice with a leopard seal."

Antarctica is quite mountainous, with peaks of over 15,000 feet, and the lure of scaling a never-before-climbed peak has attracted many adventurers. Gary Jobson was more interested in going down than climbing up, though after the first run, he decided that his skis would be better left on the boat. "I like to ski and am not at all intimidated by black-diamond runs. When we made the trip to Antarctica, I took my skis along. We landed on shore and hiked to a hill and put on crampons. We made our way to the top and I strapped on my skis. I made one turn, and soon realized I was on sheer ice. I came to a stop after a hundred yards, realizing that I could easily have gone off a cliff or into a crevasse. I put my crampons back on then and there. I still don't know how I stopped."

Gary Jobson is a world-class sailor, television commentator, and author based in Annapolis, Maryland. Gary covered the 2003 America's Cup in Auckland, New Zealand, for ESPN and *Sailing World*. In 2004 he covered the Sailing Olympics for NBC in Athens. Gary has won many championships in one-design classes, the America's Cup with Ted Turner in 1977, the infamous Fastnet Race, and many of the world's ocean races. In college he was an All American sailor three times and was twice named College Sailor of the Year (1972, 1973). In October 2003 Gary was inducted into the America's Cup Hall of

Fame by the Herreshoff Marine Museum. In 1999 he won the Nathanael G. Herreshoff Trophy, US Sailing's most prestigious award. This trophy is awarded annually to an individual who has made an outstanding contribution to the sport of sailing in the United States. Gary has been ESPN's sailing commentator since 1985. In 1988 he won an Emmy for his coverage of yachting at the Olympic Games in South Korea. Gary has authored fifteen sailing books and is editor at large of *Sailing World* and *Cruising World* magazines. Over the past twenty-five years he has given nearly two thousand lectures throughout the world. His newest book is titled *A Cat: A Century of Tradition.* Gary is the National Regatta Chairman of the Leukemia & Lymphoma Society's sailing program.

IF YOU GO

➤ **Getting There:** Pelagic Sailing Expeditions (see below) begins expeditions from Puerto Williams, Chile. Puerto Williams is served from Punta Arenas, Chile (visit www.aeroviasdap.com for details), which is in turn served from Santiago by LanChile, LanExpress, and Sky Airline. Flights to Santiago are available from most major carriers.

➤ **Best Time to Visit:** There's a limited window when the ice breaks enough around Antarctica to make a visit; it's December to March. Conditions crossing the Drake Passage—and in Antarctica, for that matter—are considered extreme. This is not a trip for the faint of heart.

➤ **Charter Operators:** Gary Jobson recommends Skip Novak's Pelagic Sailing Expeditions (www.pelagic.co.uk) for charters to Antarctica. Trips are for a minimum of 21 days, and depart from Puerto Williams, Chile. Where exactly you'll go on your expedition is dependent on weather and ice conditions; it's not uncommon to spend half of your time in Antarctica stormbound.

➤ **On-Shore Accommodations:** Tiny Puerto Williams has several options, including Hostería Camblor (+56 61 621033; hosteriacamblor@terra.cl) and the Hostal Yagan (+56 61 621334; hostalyagan@hotmail.com). Punta Arenas, a small city, has more options, including the Hotel Nogueira (+56 61 248840; www.hotelnogueira.com).

ANTIGUA

RECOMMENDED BY **Mike Sanderson**

Yachtsman extraordinaire Mike Sanderson has raced just about everywhere you can imagine. So it speaks volumes when Mike names Antigua as one of his favorite racing venues.

"I've done the Antigua Race Week a number of times," Mike began. "The sailing is spectacular—there's beautiful scenery, lovely warm water, great reliable trade winds, and great island hospitality. Antigua is very well set up for racing sailboats. The local people work very well with the visiting crews to make it as easy as possible."

Antigua is situated in the middle of the Leeward Islands, at the northeastern edge of the Caribbean. Christopher Columbus came upon the island in 1493, and it's believed that he named it—somewhat inexplicably—for a church in Seville, Spain. The pattern of European colonization of Antigua follows the script established for other Caribbean islands: England and France grappled for control of Antigua, which had potential for agricultural exploitation and a strategic location at "the gateway to the Caribbean." By the late 1600s, England had prevailed. Sugar plantations were cultivated and tended to by African slaves; more than a hundred cane-processing windmills, made of stone, still dot the island today. Slavery was abolished in 1834, and most of Antigua's citizens are descendants of slaves. Antigua joined with the nearby islands of Barbuda and Redonda to become a state of the Commonwealth in 1967, and achieved independence in 1981. While sugar and pineapples are still grown for export, Antigua increasingly relies on tourism for its economic sustenance. And there's no question that tourism reaches its apex in late April during Antigua Race Week.

Antigua Race Week had rather humble beginnings; the first race in 1967 brought ten old wooden boats to the starting line. Today, it's grown into one of the more prominent regattas in the world, with more than two hundred boats participating. Races are held at

venues including Dickenson Bay, English Harbor, and Falmouth Harbor. The race covers much of Antigua's western and southern coastline, and, in turn, it seems that the entire island throws itself into a celebration of the race. What makes Antigua different from other top-tier races is that it has a somewhat relaxed environment. Super yachts compete alongside more modest craft; America's Cup winners sail next to weekend wannabes. Even the structure of the week speaks to an emphasis on fun, rather than bloodthirsty competition. In the middle of the week there's a day off from sailing, mostly, it seems, so racers (and anyone else who cares to participate) can partake in frivolity ranging from beer races to rubber raft races. "Lay Day," as it's become known, is just one of many parties throughout the week. Another notable party is the English Harbor Rum Crew Ball, held some years at Nelson's Dockyard. (The dockyard takes its name from Admiral Lord Nelson, who was stationed here from 1784 to 1787; by all reports he hated Antigua, bitter that he was posted in the colonies when naval battles were raging in Europe.) "I've participated in the America's Cup, Volvo Races, and other very serious competitions," Mike continued. "I love Antigua because it's a chance to have a good time while doing what I love doing. It's not necessarily at the cutting edge of the racing scene, but that hardly matters."

As mentioned above, Antigua Race Week attracts a broad variety of participants. In 2006, one of the highest-profile yachts in the world made an appearance—the *Mari-Cha IV*. The *Mari-Cha IV* is a remarkable craft. Designed by five leading designers and yachtsmen (including Mike Sanderson) and built entirely of carbon fiber, it stretches 140 feet and is capable of achieving speeds of more than 40 knots. Owner Robert Miller had the *Mari-Cha IV* constructed at France's JMV boatyard with one goal in mind—to be the fastest offshore monohull ever to sail. In its very first voyage in October of 2003 the silver-hulled craft made history, crossing from New York to the U.K. in just over six days, breaking the west-to-east transatlantic speed record by two days. As of press time, the *Mari-Cha IV* has gone on to break records for the Guadalupe to Antigua Race, the Trans-Pacific Ocean Race, and the Rolex Transatlantic Challenge, and has won line honors for every contest it has participated in.

"I'll always remember one of the races at Antigua with the *Mari-Cha IV*," Mike recounted. "As the largest boat, we started last—though we weren't there for long. On one of the downwind runs, we came flying through the ranks. We passed many smaller boats in the 40-to-50-foot class. All the crew members of these boats lined up and applauded as

OPPOSITE
Antigua sailing
excitement
reaches its apex
during Antigua
Race Week in
late April.

this spectacular craft came through. Though we were in the midst of a competition, these people understood that they were seeing a world record–setting boat at the top of its form, and they understood how special that was. This tells the tale of the supportive racing atmosphere you find at Antigua."

Mike Sanderson is one of the leading all-round yachtsmen in the world today, with a background as a competitor, a sailmaker, and a designer. A native New Zealander, he has been sailing since the age of five. Mike's first major conquest came in 1993, when he served as trimmer on board the *New Zealand Endeavour*, which won the Whitbread Round the World (now the Volvo Ocean Race). Since that time, he has served as trimmer/helmsman on the *New Zealand Endeavour* as it took line honors in the Sydney-Hobart race; as watch captain and sail coordinator on the *Merit Cup*, which took second place in the 1995/96 Whitbread; as mainsheet trimmer for two America's Cup campaigns (1995 with Tag Heuer and 2003 with Oracle BMW); as watch captain onboard the *Zephyrus IV* as it set the record for the Cape Town to Rio Race; and as helmsman for the *Mari-Cha IV* when it broke the transatlantic record by over two days. In June 2006, Mike won the Volvo Ocean Race 2005–2006 aboard the *Abn Amro One*, his first Volvo Ocean Race/Whitbread round-the-world race as skipper. Mike has participated in and won countless other races.

> IF YOU GO

➤ **Getting There:** Antigua is served by many airlines from North America, including Air Canada, American, Continental, Delta, and U.S. Airways.

➤ **Best Time to Visit:** Racing enthusiasts will want to visit during Antigua Race Week, which occurs in late April/early May. Antigua's tropical climate varies little throughout the year, though there's a greater chance for rain (and hurricanes) in the fall.

➤ **Charter Operators:** Bareboat charter operations in Antigua include SunSail (888-350-3568; www.sunsail.com) and CharterWorld.com (www.charterworld.com).

➤ **Moorings:** In English Harbor, contact Antigua Slipway (268-460-1056) or Nelson's Dockyard Marina (268-481-5035). On St. John's waterfront, contact Redcliffe Quay Marina (268-462-1847).

➤ **On-Shore Accommodations:** The Antigua and Barbuda Department of Tourism (305-381-6762; www.antigua-barbuda.org) lists a broad range of lodgings options.

Australia

FREMANTLE

RECOMMENDED BY **Thomas A. Whidden**

A special race can certainly endear a place to a sailor. Especially if that race involves winning back the America's Cup. Just ask Tom Whidden.

"I'd never been to western Australia before," Tom recalled, "but in preparation for the America's Cup races in 1987, I moved my family there and enrolled my kids in school. At the time, Fremantle seemed like quite a small town. They had sheep-transport ships in the harbor, which were used to send live sheep to the Middle East. The place where we trained was originally a little fishing harbor, with quite a few fishing boats. At the beginning, I don't think they liked having us around. Slowly but surely, however, they seemed to come around and enjoy having us there. By the end of our stay, we were all friends. That was a great part of the overall experience in Fremantle."

Fremantle, Australia, is a suburb of Perth, the largest city in western Australia, which is set a dozen miles inland on the banks of the Swan River. Fremantle and nearby Rottnest Island have been prized as holiday retreats for residents of the province for years, but popularity surged after the town's facelift in preparation for the America's Cup in 1987.

Since hosting the Cup, the region has also seen more visitors from abroad. Fremantle boasts the fine climate and easygoing vibe that Americans have come to associate with Australia, along with an abundance of cafés and bistros spread along the bustling harbor, which is still home to a fishing fleet of four hundred boats.

Fremantle is blessed with a steady breeze from the Indian Ocean in the summer—dubbed the Fremantle Doctor—and is buffered from the open sea by Rottnest. These facets, combined with water that's not overly deep, make Fremantle a wonderful racing venue. "In some respects, it's reminiscent of Newport," Tom said. "Instead of having

Block Island offshore, you have Rottnest. And everyone has such a love of sailing. It's really a popular sport in Australia."

It's hard to overstate how much winning the 1987 America's Cup in Fremantle meant to the American yachting community—and to Americans in general. While the America's Cup race had been conducted since 1851, it's safe to say that it had not been part of the average American's sports lexicon. That is, until it was lost for the first time in 131 years in 1983 to the *Australia II* and a team sponsored by Australia's Fremantle Yacht Club, effectively breaking the longest winning streak in modern sports history. The loss was especially difficult for Dennis Conner, the skipper of America's yacht, *Liberty*. (There's a saying that if the America's Cup were ever lost, its place in a glass case at the New York Yacht Club would be replaced by the losing skipper's head.) Experts agree that Conner sailed especially well off Newport, Rhode Island, in 1983, but that *Australia II*'s contro-versial "winged-keel" design made it a considerably faster boat. Instead of losing his head, Conner regrouped with new backing, a new sponsoring club (San Diego Yacht Club), and a new boat, *Stars and Stripes*. The face-off in the Indian Ocean off Fremantle, where *Stars and Stripes* won four straight races over Australia's *Kookaburra III* by an aver-age margin of over one minute, sent the yachting world a resounding message—Conner and America were back! The victory earned Conner a cover feature in *Time* magazine, a sure sign that *Stars and Stripes* had been competing for a lot more than a silver cup.

"If there's a moment from a sailing perspective that stands out for me about my time in Fremantle, it would be the first race against *Kookaburra*," Tom continued. "There had been a lot of press about *Kookaburra*'s design, saying that it was a very fast boat. The winds that day were not the Fremantle Doctor from the west, but a hot wind from the mainland to the east. We started to the left of *Kookaburra*, and got the first wind shift, which gave us an immediate advantage. We were able to cover them and stay ahead, and we never looked back.

"Though I've only been back once, I have many fond remembrances of Fremantle," Tom concluded. "It was a wonderful place to live, and I would've loved to stay—except that we had a ticker tape parade awaiting us in New York, and an audience with President Reagan."

Not the kind of social obligations one should miss!

OPPOSITE

Team Kookaburra III *(shown here) was overcome by* Stars and Stripes *in the waters off Fremantle in 1987, bringing the America's Cup back to the United States.*

Thomas A. Whidden, who began sailing at age ten at the Cedar Point Yacht Club in Westport, Connecticut, is one of the most experienced America's Cup sailors in the world. He has sailed with Dennis Conner in a total of seven America's Cup campaigns, beginning in 1979, as Conner's trial-horse skipper. Tom's relationship with Conner has continued to develop over the past two decades; he has raced as tactician in five America's Cup series races and has won the Cup three times. Tom is the president and CEO of the North Marine Group (which owns North Sails, Southern Spars, and Edgewater Power Boats), a post he has held since 1996. A graduate of Colby College in Waterville, Maine, he has earned many accolades throughout his sailing career, including the Carl Nelson award from Colby College for Athletic Achievement after College in 1989 and the University Club "Man of the Year" award in 1987. Tom was given a Key to New York City from Mayor Ed Koch in 1987 after bringing the America's Cup back to the United States from Australia. He has enjoyed much sailing success outside of the America's Cup arena, having won the Bermuda Race (Class A) five times and his class at SORC five times and twice overall. Along with being an accomplished sailor and executive, Tom is the publisher and coauthor of two books, *The Art and Science of Sails* and *Championship Tactics*.

IF YOU GO

➤ **Getting There:** Fremantle is a suburb of Perth, which is served by many major carriers, including Air New Zealand, British Airways, and Qantas.

➤ **Best Time to Visit**: November through March, during the Australian spring and summer.

➤ **Charter Operators:** Few charters are available from Fremantle/Perth, though Charter One (+61 8 9339 4889; www.charter1.com.au) does offer skippered catamaran charters during the summer season.

➤ **Moorings:** Visitor's berths are available at Challenger Harbor (+61 8 9239 2481) and Aquarama Marina (+61 8 9339 5666; www.aquarama.com.au).

➤ **On-Shore Accommodations:** Fremantle is a popular getaway for Aussies, and offers a host of accommodations. For a complete listing, contact the Fremantle Visitors Centre (+61 8 9431 7878; www.fremantlewa.au.com) or Tourism Western Australia (www.western australia.com).

SYDNEY

RECOMMENDED BY **Matt Hayes**

✳

It's not a coincidence that the Sydney Opera House showcases a dramatic "sails" design. Sailing is a big-time sport here in Australia, especially on the southeast coast of the continent. And Sydney Harbor provides an ideal venue to hoist a sail.

"Sydney is one of the most dynamic cities in the world," reflected Matt Hayes, "and we're blessed with a wonderful harbor. It's one of the only natural harbors in the world where you have the central business district right on the water, and despite this—and the fact that Sydney is Australia's largest city, with over four and a half million people—the water is crystal clear and unpolluted. I've been all around the world, and I've never seen such a pristine harbor as this. It's a jewel in the collective Australian crown, and we work hard on maintaining its beauty."

Sydney Harbor (Port Jackson) is roughly 12 miles long, spreading southwest from Sydney Heads (North and South Head, respectively) to the iconic Opera House, then underneath the nearly-as-iconic Sydney Harbor Bridge, and continuing west to the suburban town of Balmain, where it mingles with the outflow of the Parramatta and Lane Cove Rivers. It's the largest natural harbor in the world, with a perimeter of nearly 200 miles. Locals think of Port Jackson as three harbors—North Harbor, Middle Harbor, and Sydney Harbor, with the latter being the largest (and what outsiders think of as Sydney). "It's a big water port," Matt continued, "with rocky outcroppings and white, sandy beaches. Despite being Australia's biggest city, it's not hard to experience isolation in the harbor." In fact, Sydney Harbor (and the coast north and south of the Heads) has some seventy beaches, and a national park—Sydney Harbor National Park—a short cruise from the central business district.

The weather in Sydney is always conducive to sailing. "We have two seasons," Matt said, "warm and quite warm. You can sail year round. October through April [spring and summer in the Southern Hemisphere], we get wonderful easterly/northeasterly breezes, though it can be hot and humid for the uninitiated. During our winter, we get a westerly land breeze. Wintertime generally brings a path of high pressure over Sydney. While it's not as windy, it's comfortably dry—really a pleasant time to be here."

For many, Sydney is synonymous with racing, and the race that sealed Sydney's reputation is the Sydney to Hobart, the most publicized sailboat race in the world next to the America's Cup and the Volvo Round the World Race. The race, sponsored by the Cruising Yacht Club of America and Rolex, has been conducted since 1945, includes boats ranging from 30 to 90 feet, and pits weekend cruisers against world-class competitive sailors. "It's hard to overstate the significance of the Sydney to Hobart Race on the Australian sporting scene," Matt said. "Next to the Melbourne Cup [Australia's premier horse race], it's our biggest sports event—something like the baseball playoffs in the States, I imagine. On Boxing Day—the day after Christmas, when the race begins—literally thousands of craft, sailboats and motorboats, follow the competitors out of the harbor. Hundreds of thousands of other spectators are on the shore. It's a tradition for boating spectators to anchor, have a seafood lunch and some nice Chardonnay, and think about the crews heading south."

By all reports, the crews participating in the 628-nautical-mile race to Tasmania need all the good wishes their spectators can muster. After leaving the well-wishers in Sydney, racers proceed down the coast of the main island. Leaving the coast, they reach the 140-odd-mile stretch of open water separating Australia from the island province of Tasmania—the Bass Strait—which can be particularly nasty thanks to shallow water and sometimes strong winds. As sailors reach Storm Bay and Tasman waters, frustrations can increase as fickle winds and complex currents can confound progress. The finishing point of Hobart, eleven miles up the Derwent River and framed by Mount Wellington, is indeed a welcome sight. A cup or two of cheer for winners and nonwinners alike (anyone who finishes the race is a winner of sorts) awaits, perhaps at the Customs House Hotel, whose pub is popular with the sailing set. "I do the Sydney to Hobart for three days," Matt added laughing. "It's my annual punishment, my penance."

If all goes well, Matt and his crewmates will grab a few pints and a few hours of sleep in Hobart before hustling back to Sydney to catch the New Year's Eve fireworks display.

OPPOSITE
Beautiful Sydney is blessed with the largest natural harbor in the world, and its inhabitants take advantage.

"Next to the start of the Sydney to Hobart Race, it's one of the main events in Sydney," Matt said. "And the best place to see the show is from a boat right on the harbor."

Matt Hayes is the owner of the award-winning Sydney By Sail (www.sydneybysail.com) charter company in Sydney, which provides a host of sailing activities to over seven thousand people each year. Matt is an Olympic sailor from Atlanta in the soling class and was ranked number four in the world in 1996. He has won numerous Australian and NSW sailing championships, and has competed in twelve Sydney to Hobart yacht races, numerous blue-water events along the eastern seaboard of Australia, and International Yachting regattas such as the Admiral's Cup and Kenwood Cup. Matt is also the importer/distributor for Hunter's Yachts throughout Australia, New Zealand, and the South Pacific.

▶ IF YOU GO ◀

➤ **Getting There:** Sydney is served by many major carriers, including Air New Zealand, British Airways, and Qantas.

➤ **Best Time to Visit:** Sydney is blessed with some 240 days of sunshine, though you'll find the warmest weather November through March.

➤ **Charter Operators:** There are a number of charter operators offering both bareboat and skippered craft, including Sydney by Sail (+61 2 9280 1110; www.sydneybysail.com) and Pittwater Yacht Charter (+61 2 9997 5344; www.yachtcharter.com.au).

➤ **Moorings:** Moorings are available from more than a dozen marinas in the Sydney area.

➤ **On-Shore Accommodations:** Tourism New South Wales (www.visitnsw.com.au) offers an exhaustive list of lodgings options in this extraordinary city.

ST. GEORGE'S HARBOR

RECOMMENDED BY **B. W. "Jordy" Walker**

Jordy Walker's family has been sailing about Bermuda for nearly 400 years. After so many generations, one could say that he's hardwired to appreciate the island's many appeals. "My ancestors—all nine generations of B. W. Walkers—were traders and sailors," Jordy explained. "They would trade stone for making chimneys to salt rakers on the Turks and Caicos, and in turn bring the salt up to the Northeast, where it would be used to cure fish. They traded the salt for vegetables, clothing, hardware, and tools, which they'd bring back to Bermuda."

Ships departing from Bermuda in those days lifted anchor from the harbor of St. George, on the north side of the island. Today, St. George's Harbor remains the island's first port of call. "There are an awful lot of people coming through," Jordy mused. "I don't know where they are going, but I do know why they come—it's for the hospitality and they seem to enjoy it."

The town of St. George dates back to 1612, making it the fifth-oldest Northern European settlement in the New World, and the oldest English town. As such, it was named a UNESCO World Heritage Site in 2000. Bermuda was discovered in 1609, when a squadron of English ships under the command of Admiral Sir George Somers wrecked near St. George, after being blown off their course for Jamestown, Virginia. It's believed that an account of the shipwreck penned by William Strachey provided fodder for Shakespeare's comedy *The Tempest*, which references "the still vexed Bermoothes" in act 1, scene 2. (The town's namesake was not its founder, but the patron saint of England, St. George.) "For all intents and purposes, the village has not changed in 200 years," Jordy said. "Some buildings are 400 years old. As customs is located here, all visiting yachts must put in. It's

customary for visitors to stop in at the Whitehorse Tavern for some fish chowder and a 'Dark and Stormy,' the national drink."

Bermuda is well known as the terminus for two blue-water contests—the Newport Bermuda Race and the Marion Bermuda Race. The Newport Bermuda Race, billed as the oldest recurring ocean race in the world and cosponsored by the Cruising Club of America and the Royal Bermuda Yacht Club, was first conducted in 1906, though it had a series of different launching points before Newport was settled on in 1936. The 635-nautical-mile race will generally take from three to six days (depending on conditions), and concludes in Hamilton on the south end of the island. The Marion Bermuda Race, a joint effort of the Beverly (MA) Yacht Club, the Blue Water Sailing Club, and the Royal Hamilton Amateur Dinghy Club, began in 1977; this slightly more low-key race is geared toward cruising yachts and family sailors, and occurs biyearly. "If you're interested in ocean racing and in seeing the biggest and best yachts, race weeks are a good time to be here," Jordy added. "Some, however, would find it a distraction, as it's hard to find accommodations. But if you enjoy talking yachting, it's a great place to be."

A unique facet of the Bermuda sailing experience is the Fitted Dinghy races, which are conducted at St. George's Harbor, Hamilton Harbor, and Mangrove Bay. "The Fitted Dinghy races are Bermuda's yachting spectator sport," Jordy said. "Beginning on May 24 and every second or third weekend thereafter, people come out in tiny boats and follow the fleet around. The dinghies only sail windward to leeward, lest they capsize. They change rigs for different weather conditions; at times, they can spend as much as 2,000 square feet of sail out. We don't race if the wind is upward of twenty knots.

"The rules of fitted dinghy racing are the oldest in the world of sailboat racing. They are rooted in commercial fishing, when boats would race to shore with their catch. When two boats are sailing to windward and converge on a collision course, the crews yell, 'Hard alee!' and both must tack. There is no right-of-way rule. Downwind passing on the 'inside' is dangerous, as the boat being overtaken can luff to windward, strike the overtaking boat, and foul it out of the race. Fitted dinghy racing has another interesting rule: no one has to be in the boat to finish the race successfully. If the wind is light, it's common practice to push a few guys off the stern, which thrusts the boat forward.

"I recall one race when our boat was in front as we approached the finish line," Jordy continued. "It looked as though we were going to win, but then another boat came close. I was the skipper, and I said, 'Okay, bow to stern, I want you guys out, one at a time, start-

OPPOSITE
Fitted dinghy
races are
a uniquely
Bermudan
racing
phenomenon.

ing with the guy at the front—number one, number two,' and so on. I finally leaped off myself, and our boat made it over! We beat the other boat by 6 inches! Our boat capsized at the finish line. It took all seven of us pushing off to win—seven torpedoes into the harbor. Then it took us an hour to right the boat, bail it dry, and re-rig for the next race. That's dinghy racing!"

B. W. "Jordy" Walker comes from a long line of Bermudan sailors. "I'll sail anything, anytime, from dinghies to ocean racing vessels, as long as a race is on!" Jordy said. He's been extremely active in the competitive sailing world for many years, holding a number of senior positions for a variety of organizations, including president of the IOD World Class Association, 1986–90; member of the ISAF Match Racing Committee, 1989–98; commodore of the Royal Bermuda Yacht Club, 1990–91; president of the Bermuda Yachting Association, 1991–94; president of the World Match Racing Conference, 1993–94; president of the Match Racing Association, 2002–04; and director of the World Match Racing Tour, 2005. In 2006, Jordy competed in the IOD Class during the Bermuda International Race Week, the 100th anniversary Newport to Bermuda Race, and the IOD World Championships. When he's not on the water, Jordy is a senior architect with OBM International Limited, a building design firm ranked in the top thirty-five resort design firms worldwide.

IF YOU GO

➤ **Getting There:** Nonstop flights are offered to Bermuda on many carriers from most major eastern U.S. cities, and from Chicago, Toronto, Halifax, and London.

➤ **Best Time to Visit:** If you're interested in racing, Bermuda's racing season runs from March to November. As Jordy Walker mentioned, the island's ports tend to be quite crowded during the major races that conclude here, most of which are held in June.

➤ **Charter Operators:** A number of businesses rent small sailboats (Lasers/Sunfish) or offer skippered day charters; they are listed at www.bermudatourism.com.

➤ **Moorings:** The following offer moorings to visiting sailors: Captain Smokes Marina in St. George's (441-297-1940); St. George's Boatyard (441-297-0877); Dockyard Marina in Sandys Parish (441-234-0300); and West End Yachts in Sandys (441-234-1303).

➤ **On-Shore Accommodations:** Bermuda (www.bermudatourism.com) offers a list of lodgings options, from bed-and-breakfasts to resort hotels.

BAY OF ILHA GRANDE

RECOMMENDED BY **Lin Pardey**

Some of Brazil's treasures—the nightlife of Rio de Janeiro, the beach at Ipanema—are well known by international travelers. But others have been less publicized, perhaps to save them for Brazilians . . . that is, until Lin Pardey came along.

"We were in Cape Town, and there were only a few other foreign yachts there," Lin recalled. "One housed a Brazilian family who was finishing a round-the-world voyage. They asked where we were headed next, and we said 'Norway.' 'You must come to Brazil, then!' the father exclaimed. 'It's on the easiest and most pleasurable route to Europe.' I happened to call my parents in the States shortly thereafter and mentioned the potential of going to Brazil, and my mother remarked, 'Then you'll probably go to Rio de Janeiro.' I asked why, and my mother reminded me that I had cousins there. I wrote them a letter and mentioned that we might be coming through, and they wrote right back, informing us that they had a berth ready for us. 'We want to take you to Ilha Grande,' they said. The Brazilian family gave us all of their local charts, and we were soon on our way.

"When we got to Rio, we saw another side of life. It turns out that my cousins are quite wealthy. They have a penthouse that looks out over the city and the waterfront. My cousins described Ilha Grande as a beautiful and wonderful place that was quite different from Rio, though it possesses a distinctive Brazilian flavor. They were right on all counts."

The Bay of Ilha Grande is approximately a hundred miles south of Rio de Janeiro—a day and a half's sail for Lin and her entourage—in the district known as Angra dos Reis. The bay takes its name from Ilha Grande, the largest of the 360 islands that rise in the bay. The island has a colorful and somewhat nefarious history. When Spaniards discovered silver and gold in Peru toward the end of the sixteenth century, pirates would lie in wait around Ilha Grande, hoping to intercept Spanish ships. Later, when mining operations and coffee plantations were established on the mainland and created an increased demand for labor, millions of slaves were brought to Brazil. Ilha Grande was then a haven for slavers. In the early 1900s, with slavery out of fashion, the island was selected as the place for a penal colony, and later a prison. In 1994 the prison was officially closed, and much of the island was designated as a nature sanctuary. "It's my sense that Ilha Grande is a Brazilian playground," Lin commented. "Not many foreigners know about it, or bother to make the trip here."

The Bay of Ilha Grande, which has been dubbed the "Caribbean of Brazil" by some, offers visitors tremendous diversity. There are tropical jungles, replete with howling monkeys, that suggest the interior regions of the Amazon; parts of Ilha Grande and segments of the mainland coast make up the most intact Mata Atlántica (Atlantic Rainforest) left in the world. Adjoining these thick canopies are beautiful, white beaches bordered by crystal-clear waters, where colorful fish swim in tremendous schools. (Lopes Mendes is considered by many to be one of the most beautiful beaches in all Brazil.) On the mainland are interesting villages to explore. "Considering the proximity of Rio and São Paulo [which together harbor some 30 million souls], Ilha Grande is refreshingly uncrowded," Lin said, "especially during the week. It's very well suited for cruising—we could stay in a quiet place for a week and have a bay almost to ourselves, and then find an interesting place to go ashore and explore. The only drawback to Ilha Grande is the fact that there are very light winds. You can't count on finding exciting sailing here."

On the southern edge of the Bay of Ilha Grande is the town of Parati. "Parati was at the end of the Gold Trail (Caminho do Ouro)," continued Lin. "Any miners coming from the interior had to pass through. The gold trade at the end of the seventeenth century—and the farming and processing of sugar cane—helped make Parati one of the wealthiest cities in the world. Much of Parati was built too close to the sea, and at high tide, streets are submerged; drainage was finally built in. There are beautiful old stone houses there that were built from the rocks used for ballast in trading ships."

One of the special endearments of cruising Ilha Grande is the chance to partake of a meal from a floating restaurant. Several such establishments—Barco Bar and Jango's Bar—are anchored off Ilha de Gipoia, near a spot called Dentist's Beach. "You can order food over your radio, or someone from the restaurant will come by and take your order," Lin recalled. "You can eat at the restaurant/bar, which is a flat-bottomed boat. Or a lady in a very brief bikini will deliver the food back to your boat. It's a very popular spot."

Lin Pardey was born in Detroit, Michigan, and raised in Los Angeles County. She began sailing on lakes around Michigan in a 14-foot Old Town Sloop at the age of five. She met her husband-to-be, Larry, in 1965, and since that time, they've sailed hundreds of thousands of miles together around the world. Their many books include *Storm Tactics Handbook; Cruising in Seraffyn; Seraffyn's European Adventure; Seraffyn's Mediterranean Adventure; Seraffyn's Oriental Adventure; The Self-sufficient Sailor; The Capable Cruiser; The Care and Feeding of Sailing Crew; Details of Classic Boat Construction: The Hull;* and *Cost Conscious Cruiser*. Lin and Larry's DVDs include *Storm Tactics, Get Ready to Cruise,* and *Get Ready to Cross Oceans*. Their articles have appeared in countless periodicals, including *Sail* magazine, *Cruising World*, and *Woodenboat*. You can read their newsletters at www.landlpardey.com. Lin and Larry have also received many honors, including the International Oceanic Award, presented by the Royal Institute of Navigation; the Ocean Cruising Club Award, for contributions to seamanship for small-boat sailing; the Ocean Cruising Club Merit Award, for inspiring voyages including a west-about rounding of Cape Horn; and the Seven Seas Cruising Club Service Award, for their lifetime voyaging achievements. Lin and Larry were inducted into the Cruising World Hall of Fame in 2000.

IF YOU GO

➤ **Getting There:** Ilha Grande can be reached from Rio de Janeiro, which is served by a number of carriers, including American, Continental, Delta, and United Airlines. Those not sailing from Rio will want to travel by car or bus to the town of Angra dos Reis.

➤ **Best Time to Visit:** Ilha Grande enjoys a tropical climate tempered by cooling winds. While the weather is warm year round, there's less rainfall between December and March.

➤ **Charter Operators:** Several charters are available in Rio, including Orion Yachts (www. orionyachts.com.br) and Brazil Yacht Charter (www.byc.com.br).

➤ **On-Shore Accommodations:** The Brazilian Tourism Office (800-727-2945; www. braziltourism.org) has lodgings information for Rio, Angra dos Reis, and Ilha Grande.

CHANNEL ISLANDS

RECOMMENDED BY **J. J. Isler**

"My family has been sailing over to Catalina from San Diego every year since I was a baby," J. J. Isler recalled. "With our first boat, a heavy wooden craft that was 30 feet long, it would sometimes take twenty hours. I think my parents had me so they had one more set of hands available to help sand the varnished wood on the boat. It's been very special for me to go back there each summer, especially now with my own kids, to take them snorkeling to see the Garibaldi, and show them my secret childhood spots. My dad does the same thing with my kids that my granddad did with me."

Catalina is one of the Channel Islands, an archipelago of eight islands that rest off the southern coast of California. The Channels stretch 160 miles, from San Miguel in the north (about 60 miles due west of Ventura) to San Clemente in the south (70 miles northwest of San Diego). San Miguel, Anacapa, Santa Cruz, and Santa Rosa are collectively known as the Northern Islands, and San Nicolas, Santa Barbara, and Santa Catalina as the Southern Islands. The four Northern Islands, plus Santa Barbara, make up the Channel Islands National Park.

The character of the Channels varies greatly. San Miguel is exposed to harsh open ocean conditions, where 50-mile-per-hour winds are common, and a rock-riddled coastline makes navigation a tricky proposition. For these reasons, San Miguel sees fewer than three hundred visitors most years. On the other end of the scale, Santa Catalina (usually shortened to Catalina) sees more than one million visitors annually, largely because of its 20-odd-mile proximity to a little town called Los Angeles, regular ferry service, and plentiful tourist attractions. Of the eight islands, only Catalina has what might be termed a town—Avalon.

44

Before the arrival of Europeans, Catalina was home for various indigenous peoples who lived primarily from what they could harvest from the sea, as the island was too arid to support any agriculture. It's believed that island residents in the millennium before colonization—people from the Takic linguistic tradition, who called Catalina Pimu, and themselves Pimungans—traveled regularly to the mainland, where they would trade abalone and other sea goods for things they couldn't procure on the island. The European settlement of Catalina follows the basic script that characterizes so much of California's colonization: Spaniards discovered the island (in 1542 and again in 1602), Russians and Americans exploited it for the fur trade, and eventually Americans settled it, grazing the island's scant vegetation with small herds of sheep and cattle. Toward the end of the nineteenth century, the tourist potential for the island began to be realized, as 50,000-odd Angelenos began seeking a spot to rusticate. The small settlement on Avalon Bay expanded through the early 1900s, and development was accelerated by the purchase of the island by William Wrigley Jr. (of gum and Chicago Cubs fame), and capped off by the construction of the grand Casino, a dance hall and movie theater, in 1929.

Avalon and its tourist diversions are but a small part of Catalina Island. Almost 90 percent of the island is undeveloped and preserved through the Santa Catalina Island Conservancy, providing habitat for several animal and plant species that are found nowhere else in the world, including Catalina Island fox, Beechey ground squirrel, Catalina Island quail, Catalina manzanita, and Catalina mahogany. Hiking around Catalina's broad interior valleys, you may be somewhat surprised to come across an unlikely species—namely bison! In 1924, fourteen bison were brought to Catalina for the film adaptation of Zane Grey's novel *The Vanishing American*. When the production wrapped, it was decided that the buffalo could stay, and they remain today. Over the years the herd has been periodically supplemented and culled to preserve its overall health, and now it numbers around four hundred head.

"When we go to Catalina, we spend very little time around Avalon," J. J. continued. "We'll moor the boat at Cherry Cove near Two Harbors at the west end of the Island, and spend our days kayaking, snorkeling, fishing, and just relaxing. Back when they were more plentiful, we'd dive for abalone. We'll also go on shore for hikes. I've lived in southern California all of my life, and it's amazing to me how much it's changed. Catalina is different, however. Thanks to the Catalina Island Conservancy, it really hasn't changed at all, even though it's just twenty miles from a major metropolis."

DESTINATION 8

J. J. has spent time at several of the Channel Islands. "Sometimes on the trip back to San Diego, we'd anchor off of San Clemente (not the former home of Richard Milhouse Nixon, which is on the mainland) to go diving," she recalled. "It's owned by the U.S. Navy, and going there was always a little scary—you should check with the Navy to make sure military exercises are not going to be conducted. But my favorite Channel Island sail is the 3- or 4-hour cruise from Santa Barbara to Santa Cruz Island. We usually spend a few nights anchored off Santa Cruz exploring the caves and then have a nice sail to Catalina."

Santa Cruz (Spanish for Sacred Cross) is the largest of the Channel Islands, with almost a hundred square miles of land consisting of two mountain ranges, which form a central valley, and nearly 80 miles of coastline. The island's name has an interesting origin—it's said that a priest's staff was left on the island accidentally during the Spanish expedition of 1769, led by Gaspar de Portolá. An islander from the Chumash tribe came upon the staff and returned it to the expedition, greatly impressing the Spaniards and earning the island its name. Thanks in part to regular availability of fresh water, Santa Cruz supports a great diversity of plant species (over 650), eight of which are endemic to the island. The island's location near the boundary of colder northern and warmer southern waters makes for a rich array of marine mammal life.

There are several prominent sea caves on Santa Cruz Island, including the Painted Cave. This cave is almost a quarter mile long and stretches to widths of 100 feet, with a ceiling that reaches 160 feet. The "painting" comes from the rich colors of the rocks, algae, and lichen that grace the cave's walls. "They're so large, you can easily take a dinghy in there," J. J. said. "My kids get a little scared when we visit, as it's very dark inside and there are usually seals swimming about."

J. J. Isler has won two Olympic medals in sailing in the Women's 470 Class (bronze in 1992 and silver in 2000) and is the first female inductee into the Sailing World Hall of Fame. She is a four-time Rolex Yachtswoman of the Year and has won three world championships and numerous national and European championships. J. J. and her husband, Peter, are coauthors of *Sailing for Dummies*.

IF YOU GO

➤ **Getting There:** The Channel Islands can be most easily reached from Los Angeles, though they are accessible from anywhere in southern California. Several ferry services provide transportation to Catalina, including Catalina Tours (866-620-3724; www.catalinatours.net)

➤ **Best Time to Visit:** Catalina experiences fairly moderate temperatures year round, though the warmest months are June through October; December through February sees more precipitation.

➤ **Charter Operators:** There are a number of bareboat charter operators around Los Angeles, including Bluewater Sailing (310-823-5545; www.bluewatersailing.com) in Marina del Rey, and Marina Sailing (800-262-7245; www.marinasailing.com), which operates in six southern California cities.

➤ **Moorings:** The Harbor Department of Avalon (on Catalina Island) can be reached at 310-510-0535 or via e-mail at harborpatrol@cityofavalon.com.

➤ **On-Shore Accommodations:** The town of Avalon on Catalina Island offers a broad range of lodgings options which are highlighted by the Catalina Island Chamber of Commerce (310-510-1520; www.catalinachamber.com).

DESTINATION

8

SAN FRANCISCO BAY

RECOMMENDED BY **Glenn Isaacson**

The Golden Gate Bridge is the foremost icon in a city of icons, spanning one and three-quarter miles across the strait that bears its name. For first-time visitors and San Franciscans alike, its brilliant vermillion towers are ever awe-inspiring. For sailors, it's just another attraction of the San Francisco Bay.

"There are three words that define sailing on the San Francisco Bay for me," Glenn Isaacson said. "Intense, exciting, and exhilarating. In the Bay, you have very strong winds, powerful tides and currents, frequently inclement weather conditions, and abundant commercial traffic. With this combination, navigating the Bay is no walk in the park; it's not carefree T-shirt-and-shorts sailing. If you're able to sail at the head of the pack here, it means that you've figured out the tides and currents, have respected them, and have attained a certain level of boat-handling expertise. It's a conquering kind of experience. That's where the exhilaration comes in. There, and in the incredible and diverse beauty sailors can encounter in such a compact space."

It's estimated that 40 percent of California's water drains to the Pacific through the San Francisco Bay, via the Sacramento and San Joaquin Rivers, and a few other named bays along the way. If you include Suisun Bay, San Pablo Bay, the other waters of the Sacramento Delta, plus various wetlands in the equation, San Francisco Bay comprises some 1,600 square miles. If you look at the main part of the Bay—from the Golden Gate around to Marin County on the north end, down to San Jose in the south, and curving up to the city of San Francisco on its western edge—the Bay is a more modest 400 square miles (though as various wetlands are either developed or restored, even this number is in constant fluctuation). The Bay has four significant islands—Angel Island, across from the Marin town of Tiburon; Yerba Buena Island, which bifurcates the spans of the Bay

OPPOSITE
Racers near the Golden Gate experience brisk winds, strong currents, and incredible scenery.

Bridge; Treasure Island, a manmade landmass north of Yerba Buena that was created to host the 1939 World's Fair; and, most infamous of all, Alcatraz, a chilly one-and-a-quarter-mile swim from Fisherman's Wharf. (By the way, it's the 50-degree water and strong currents, not man-eating sharks, that made the venture from "The Rock" to the mainland so harrowing for would-be escapees.)

While not a few explorers (including Sir Francis Drake) plied the waters off northern California in search of the Northwest Passage, the strait of Golden Gate and the sheltered waters within went undiscovered by Europeans until 1769. Even then, the Bay was observed from land by a crew led by Gaspar de Portola, who, short on water and food, had moored his ship near present-day Pacifica and begun working his way overland. (The strait was likely occluded by persistent fog.) A few years later, another Spaniard, Juan de Ayala, became the first European to sail into the Bay, anchoring near Angel Island, where a cove is named in his honor. It's interesting to note that the strait that would become known as the Golden Gate did not gain its name from the Gold Rush that helped establish San Francisco as the capital of the West. Instead, it was coined "Chrysopylae" by John Fremont, a captain with the topographical engineers of the U.S. Army. In 1846, he likened the strait to a harbor in Istanbul named Chrysoceras or Golden Horn.

As Glenn mentioned above, there are several facets of San Francisco Bay that are of great interest to sailors. The first is the wind, which can average a blustery 22 to 27 knots in the summer months. At this time, the wind is abetted by unrelenting high temperatures in California's Central Valley, which form the rising air thermal systems that bring the wind—and at times the fog—screaming through the Golden Gate. The vagaries of the wind can also generate myriad microclimates; cruisers anchored up in Raccoon Strait behind Angel Island might be taking a dip to cool off while racers a mile or so west off Sausalito might be in a 55-degree fog-induced drizzle!

The second factor that Bay Area sailors must grapple with is the immense tidal current, which can reach 7 knots on an outgoing tide; scientists have pointed out that the flow of water through the Golden Gate, at 2.3 million cubic feet per second, is more than twice that of the Mississippi River as it enters the Gulf of Mexico. "There are times when the flow of the outgoing tide at the Golden Gate is so great that it exceeds the speed that a boat can attain," Glenn shared. "It's not uncommon to see boats under full sail trying to come into the Bay, either standing still or going backward. If they're not forewarned, guests unfamiliar with this aspect of Bay sailing can be quite traumatized." Traumatized indeed, considering that few anchorages are available to the north or south, and that due west all that awaits them before Asia are the Farallon Islands, made infamous by a National Geographic segment featuring the many great white sharks that frequent the islands' coastline during elephant-seal mating season. As writer Chris Caswell points out in a story on *Boats.com*, "It's no wonder that San Francisco skippers find their pleasures on the inland side of the mighty orange bridge."

Given these rather daunting challenges, it's a wonder that any but the most talented sailors take to the waters of the Bay. One gift San Francisco Bay has bestowed on the sailing community is the shelter that the Marin Headlands provide from ocean swells. If the winds get too unruly for your taste, you can always duck into Sausalito or Tiburon or behind Angel Island and wait for things to calm down.

Home to a number of yacht clubs, including the prestigious St. Francis and San Francisco Yacht Clubs, San Francisco Bay has a vibrant racing community. But the region's beautiful and varied terrain makes the Bay ideal cruising grounds as well. When asked to serve up a sample itinerary, Glenn was happy to oblige. "Let's assume that we have a typical summer day—strong winds and choppy water. After checking the tides to get a sense of how the currents would be running, I'd set up a counterclockwise tour. We'd start in Belvedere at the San Francisco Yacht Club, where I keep my boat. We'd head west to Sausalito, and then south across the entrance of the Golden Gate so we can experience the beauty of the headlands and the grandeur of the bridge. The Golden Gate has to be one of the most awe-inspiring entrances in the world. Next, we'd sail eastward downwind along the city front of San Francisco. First we'd have the wooded Presidio Park, then the fine homes of Pacific Heights, then we'd tuck in around Fisherman's Wharf to visit the sea lions at Pier Thirty-nine. Next it would be the tall towers of the Financial District; we might even go as far south as Giants Stadium, especially if a game is on. We'd then head further east to Treasure Island, where we'll often find a colony of harbor seals. The Oakland and Berkeley Hills unfold before us as we head north and tuck behind Angel Island for some warmer weather before we head up Raccoon Strait, returning to Belvedere.

"In a three- or four-hour cruise, you get all this variety—Riviera-like Marin, a state park like Angel Island, the high-rise city of San Francisco, and the industrial part of the city of Oakland. It's mind-altering. I've been sailing here for forty-five years. Every time I go out, I learn something new. On a good day, I feel that I'm on almost equal terms with the Bay."

Glenn Isaacson has been a member of the San Francisco Yacht Club since 1967, where he has served as a director. As a sailor, he is best known for around-the-buoys closed-course racing in an Express 37, *Re-Quest*, and his current boat, *Q*, a custom 40-foot day sailer designed by Carl Schumacher. In 1985 he sailed *Re-Quest* to a PHRF record for the Long Beach to Cabo race; that record stands today. When he's not on the water, Glenn is an internationally recognized real-estate development management expert. His distinguished career includes forty years of public and private real-estate development, consulting, and urban renewal. Currently a principal and CEO at Conversion Management Associates, Inc., he also has served as deputy director of the San Francisco Redevelopment Agency. His projects include the development of Oakland's City Center and Jack London Square, successful presentation of the Lucasfilm proposal to San Francisco's Presidio Trust, and completion of the new Lucasfilm Headquarters Ranch in Marin.

IF YOU GO

➤ **Getting There:** San Francisco, Oakland, and San Jose are served by most major air carriers.

➤ **Best Time to Visit:** Some of the strongest winds of the year occur in the summer months, and some of the nicest weather is in the early fall (though if you sail off Marin County you'll see the sun and warm weather spring through fall).

➤ **Charter Operators:** Nearly twenty charter businesses operate around San Francisco Bay (mostly in Marin and the East Bay), offering both bareboat and skippered craft. BoatingSF.com (www.boatingsf.com) has a comprehensive list.

➤ **Moorings:** There are more than forty marinas and a good number of sheltered anchorages in the central San Francisco Bay. BoatingSF.com (www.boatingsf.com) offers excellent information on marinas, more isolated mooring spots, and other points of interest for sailors visiting the region.

➤ **On-Shore Accommodations:** A good place to start your planning is the San Francisco Convention and Visitors Bureau (415-974-6900; www.sfvisitor.org).

CAPE HORN

RECOMMENDED BY **Amanda Swan Neal**

Few waters inspire such awe and fear among sailors as Cape Horn. Situated at the southernmost tip of South America, Cape Horn was a pivotal point in the Drake Passage, the most popular trade route for ships passing between the Atlantic and the Pacific from the 1700s to the early 1900s. Today, most commercial ships opt for the Panama Canal over the Drake Passage, and for good reason. Relentless gales, rollercoaster seas, and marauding icebergs have made the cape renowned as a graveyard for even the most competent sailors. In recent times, Cape Horn has become the province of adventurers and competitive racers. Amanda Neal is a bit of both.

"I grew up in New Zealand in a sailing family, and as a Kiwi, I was always aware of Cape Horn," Amanda Neal said. "To navigate the cape was—and is—a feather in every sailor's cap. The first opportunity I had to do so came in 1989, as part of the first all-female boat to participate in the Whitbread Round the World Race, now the Volvo Ocean Race."

The Whitbread Race, which was inaugurated in 1973, developed from discussions at the Royal Naval Sailing Association a few years earlier. After the London-based brewery Whitbread signed on as a sponsor, seventeen yachts departed from Portsmouth, England, on the first-ever global-crewed yacht race. Records from the first race recount that some participant crafts "were no different from many of the three thousand spectator boats that set out to witness the historic start. Crews were mostly adventure-driven novices, with limited experience of offshore sailing and absolutely no idea what lay ahead over the coming 27,500 nautical miles." (One enterprising sailor, Roddy Ainslie, put together a crew of twelve paying passengers, who covered costs for launching and supporting *Second Life* on its journey.) During the race, three sailors were lost overboard; a Mexican ship, *Sayula II*, was the first victor, finishing the four legs of the original course in 133 days and 13 hours.

When Tracy Edwards, who had served as cook on the *Atlantic Privateer* (a Whitbread competitor in 1985), assembled an all-woman crew (and secured funding from the king of Jordan), some in the yachting community were skeptical about whether the crew would even finish the race. But the *Maiden*'s crew proved their naysayers wrong, winning two legs of the race in class.

"That year, the cape marked the three-quarter point in the journey," Amanda continued. "Approaching the cape, we were quite thrilled. Reaching this point, we'd achieved what we'd set out to do. Being the first girl boat to round the cape, there was some media excitement. Press helicopters were supposed to come out and capture the moment for posterity. Regrettably, we didn't get the heavy ocean winds that we'd anticipated and our boat was heavy—so we didn't do as well as we would have liked. By the time we got there, the race and media entourage had moved on. We popped the one bottle of Champagne we had on board and split it between twelve crew members. I remember being very demoralized when we sailed around the island that marks the actual cape without being able to land."

Cape Horn takes its name from the city of Horn in the Netherlands; an expedition sponsored by the city fathers was launched in 1615 to explore the Drake Passage in an attempt to break the monopoly the Dutch East India Company (who used the Strait of Magellan to the north) held on Far Eastern trade. While a ship of the same name was lost off Patagonia, the name was reserved for what the expedition believed to be the southernmost tip of mainland South America. In actuality, the cape is not on the mainland, but on an island of the same name. It falls under the provenance of the Antarctica Chilean Province, and the Chilean army maintains a small presence on the island.

The fierce winds around the cape are one factor that makes sailing the Drake Passage so precarious. The winds in the latitudes below 40 degrees South are not obstructed by land; as you move further south—below 50 and 60 degrees (Cape Horn rests at 56 degrees South latitude)—they get worse. Their intensity is hastened by the relatively narrow space—about 400 miles—they must pass through in the Drake Passage, which stretches from the cape to the northern tip of the South Shetland Islands of Antarctica. The winds abet the cape's second obstacle—large waves that can reach heights of 65 feet (rogue waves up to 100 feet have been reported!). It's no wonder that in earlier times, sailors who successfully rounded the Horn were allowed to adorn their left ear with a gold hoop earring—the left ear, as it faced the Horn on an eastbound passage.

OPPOSITE
Sailors who passed the Horn going eastward commemorated their passage with a gold hoop earring on their left ear.

10

DESTINATION

In 1994, Amanda was finally able to reach land at the cape, and has spent more time there since. "You pull into a bay at the bottom of a lighthouse and tie up to a mooring buoy, drop your dinghy, and row to a beautiful beach with dark granite rocks the size of your hand. There's a lovely path and stairs built by the Chilean army that leads up to the lighthouse keeper's hut, which is tied down by wires to keep it from blowing away. The lighthouse keeper and his family are the only residents on the island. There's a little chapel by the hut. A bit farther on along a boardwalk, you reach a monument to the many sailors who have perished trying to go around the Horn. It's in the shape of an albatross and looks south. As the sun shifts, the colors of the sculpture change."

Amanda Swan Neal grew up cruising the Pacific with her family. Upon returning to Auckland she became New Zealand's first woman apprentice sail maker. Amanda's 196,000 ocean miles include a world circumnavigation as rigger aboard the *Maiden*, the first all-woman Whitbread race boat. In addition to her offshore racing and sail making, Amanda has been a tall-ship trainer and a coach for women's sailing teams. She has instructed sailors in open-sea sailing techniques aboard the *Mahina Tiare II* and *III* with her husband, John, since 1994, and is the author of *The Essential Galley Companion*.

> **IF YOU GO**

➤ **Getting There:** Pelagic Sailing Expeditions (see below) begins expeditions from Puerto Williams, Chile. Puerto Williams is served from Punta Arenas, Chile (visit www. aeroviasdap.com for details), which is in turn served from Santiago by LanChile, LanExpress, and Sky Airline. Flights to Santiago are available from most major carriers.
➤ **Best Time to Visit:** September to May. Weather conditions can be quite mercurial, with T-shirt weather shifting quickly to snow; mean temperature is in the low fifties.
➤ **Charter Operators:** Pelagic Sailing Expeditions (www.pelagic.co.uk) runs trips that visit Cape Horn, as well as the Beagle Channel and Patagonia. Trips are for a minimum of 14 days, and depart from Puerto Williams, Chile.
➤ **On-Shore Accommodations:** Tiny Puerto Williams has several options, including Hostería Camblor (+56 61 621033; hosteriacamblor@terra.cl) and the Hostal Yagan (+56 61 621334; hostalyagan@hotmail.com). Punta Arenas, a small city, has more options, including the Hotel Nogueira (+56 61 248840; www.hotelnogueira.com).

China

HONG KONG

RECOMMENDED BY **George Strome**

Most historians would agree that during the old colonial days, the British took a bit more from the nations they colonized than they brought. But they did bring some things, especially in the world of sport: to New Zealand, they introduced rugby; to India, cricket and golf.

And to Hong Kong they brought competitive sailing, a pastime that still thrives today, most notably in the activities of the Royal Hong Kong Yacht Club. "The Club has an extensive racing program in Victoria Harbor," said George Strome, who arrived in Hong Kong from Canada some thirty-four years ago for a job and, like many expatriates, has stayed on through many exciting eras. "During our racing season, from September to May, there are ten different classes racing in the harbor or outlying areas on most Saturday afternoons, and several offshore races each year. Getting out on the water is a great break from the pressures of life in Hong Kong, as you might imagine! With its setting in the harbor, activity on the water, and ambience of postrace socializing in the main bar, many overseas visitors have declared the Royal Hong Kong Yacht Club one of the best in the world."

The Special Administrative Region of Hong Kong is on the southeastern coast of China. Its strategic location has made it an important trading region that continues to be a hub of international commerce. Before the return of the colony to China in 1997, there were some concerns about what the future under Chinese rule might hold, but business has continued much as it was before the handover, in line with China's own economic development. Hong Kong became a colony of the British crown in 1843 after forces from Great Britain prevailed in a conflict called the Opium Wars, which involved a complex blend of tea, silver, and opium trading. Yacht racing began just six years later when the

Victoria Regatta Club held its first meeting. The Royal Hong Kong Yacht Club would come into being in 1894, when it was granted its royal charter, and since 1938 has been at its present location on Kellett Island, where it was built on the foundation of the former naval powder magazine. *HMS Vengeance* reopened the club after "liberating" it from Japanese occupation in September 1945. Thanks to Hong Kong's insatiable growth, Kellett Island is no longer an island, as the waters separating it from Hong Kong have been filled. However, it still retains the last bit of natural rocky coastline on the Hong Kong Island side of central Victoria Harbor.

Victoria Harbor, the natural deepwater haven that fronts Hong Kong's vertigo-inducing cityscape, is infamous for its frenetic pace. "It's not the plethora of small junks that people might picture from yesteryear," George explained. "In the harbor, there's lots of ferry traffic bringing residents to and fro, plus small Chinese coastal ships that are quite often a bit worse for wear. On the weekends, you'll find many pleasure craft making their way to island anchorages outside the harbor. If you move to the south of Hong Kong Island into Lama Channel, there's a constant flow of huge container ships. It's not unusual to see three, four, or five container ships coming in at once, as Lama Channel is nearly as busy as the Strait of Malacca to the west of Singapore. You have to pick your way across the traffic and shipping lanes very carefully when racing and cruising in these areas." While a cruise around Victoria Harbor might not be exactly relaxing, most visitors come away impressed. "When we race or do a casual sail from Kellett Island, which is in the middle of town, visitors are wowed. It gives a really amazing perspective of the cityscape all around the harbor."

The most popular local sailing event is the Round the Island Race, which occurs in mid-November. "It's about twenty-six miles around," George said, "and we get all classes of boats, with an entry of some 180 boats. In races in the early 1990s even windsurfers were allowed, but nowadays there is too much commercial traffic to accommodate them and smaller dinghies." For the keen racers, one of the highlights of the Hong Kong racing scene is the annual offshore race to the Philippines, usually in late March or April. The South China Sea Race, which has been run each even year since 1962, now sails 585 nautical miles from Kellett Island to Subic Bay, the former U.S. naval base north of Manila Bay. In odd years since 1981, a more casual cruisers' race of some 480 nautical miles has been run to San Fernando in La Union province in the north of Luzon Island. Both events are run in conjunction with the Royal Offshore Racing Club of London.

Since 1993 the Club has run the China Coast Race Week in October, when the strong northeast monsoon sets in. This has been a popular series for racing yachts and cruisers and now includes an offshore race: in odd years, to Sanya in Hainan Island, a distance of 350 nautical miles; in even years, to Nga Trang in Vietnam, a distance of 650 nautical miles. Both races are usually an excitingly fast downhill spinnaker ride. Chinese ports are slowly opening up to recreational sailing, and more races along the coast, to Shanghai, and to Qindao are expected in the lead-up to the 2008 Olympics in China.

Other groups and clubs also fill the local sailing calendar with well-subscribed events. Each year the local cruiser owners' association runs three or four two-legged races to and from Macau, the former Portuguese colony on the west bank of the Pearl River. These races are usually over long weekends, allowing those interested to check out the fine local restaurants and imported wine stocks, or to visit casinos and glitzy new Las Vegas–style resorts. In the summer months, Hebe Haven Yacht Club runs the very popular Typhoon Series on six alternate Sundays in the Port Shelter area, plus the Mirs Bay Race, which gets the boats up to verdant cruising areas in the far northeast waters of Hong Kong. On alternate Sundays Aberdeen Sailing Club, based on the south side of Hong Kong Island in the famous fishing port and floating seafood restaurant area, runs a summer series. "We affectionately call it the restaurant series," George said, "as most of the races finish at or near an island village with a visit to a local seafood restaurant, where most of the competing parties convene after the race. It's usually one or two hours of intense and hot summer racing, then three or four hours of discussion about the race over good cold beer and a fine seafood meal."

Hong Kong is not without its cruising grounds; the region's many islands provide a respite from the pace of Victoria Harbor. "To the southeast, there is Po Toi Island," George continued. "Ming Kee seafood restaurant is a rustic but fine family-run establishment there that many sailors like to visit on a Sunday cruise. If you sail up the east coast, most of the area is pristine country park; the green, rugged coastline is an amazing contrast to the skyscrapers surrounding the harbor, often just on the other side of those green hills. Once you get up to Mirs Bay, there is good cruising toward Tolo Harbor, and the enclosed Double Haven area is a favorite for weekend cruising and really getting away from it all."

If one had only a few hours to be on the water in Hong Kong and wanted to experience a spectacle that encapsulates the hubbub of the place, you could do no better than to set

11

DESTINATION

sail on Victoria Harbor in the evening to take in the sunset and *The Symphony of Lights*. Each evening at eight o'clock (weather permitting), major buildings on both sides of the harbor come ablaze with colored lights and laser beams that pulsate in time to a synchronized thirteen-minute soundtrack that is broadcast over the water.

George Strome is a Canadian architect from Kitchener-Waterloo, Ontario, where as a young lad he sailed in dinghies at summer camp in Georgian Bay. George went to Hong Kong in 1972 on a two-year contract. Friends introduced him to sailing in Hong Kong. In 1974 he crewed on a Hustler 30 in the South China Sea Race to Manila; he has since raced some twenty times and cruised six times across these waters. George has been a keen sailor in the Sonata Class at the Royal Hong Kong Yacht Club, crewing since 1980 and helming his own Sonata *Chopstix* since 1989 in class racing and club pursuit events in the harbor. In 1995–99 he was the club sailing secretary and was very involved with the race committees for offshore races to the Philippines and along the China Coast. He has also crewed on many larger racing boats, and since August 2000 has done extensive cruising and passages in the South China Sea and the South Pacific on the legendary *Intrigue* out of New Zealand, Australia, and to and from Hong Kong. He has also participated in many regional regattas, including the King's Cup Regatta in Phuket, Thailand; Raja Muda Regattas along the west coast of Malaysia; and the President's Cup Regattas in the Philippines.

◄ IF YOU GO ►

➤ **Getting There:** Hong Kong is served by most international air carriers, including Delta, United, Northwest, and Cathay Pacific.

➤ **Best Time to Visit:** Hong Kong has a subtropical monsoon climate; fall is the best time to visit, with conditions sunny and less humid than at other times of the year.

➤ **Charter Operators:** There aren't any charter operators to speak of in greater Hong Kong, though if you wish to crew for a day, opportunities are often available at local clubs, including the Royal Hong Kong Yacht Club (+852 2832 2817; www.rhkyc.org.hk).

➤ **Moorings:** Hong Kong has excellent services for visiting yachts, and many berthing options, including Discovery Bay Marina (+852 2987 9591; www.dbyc.net).

➤ **On-Shore Accommodations:** A broad variety of lodgings options are listed at the Hong Kong Tourism Board (www.discoverhongkong.com).

LAKE DILLON

RECOMMENDED BY **Nick Iwaskow**

Sometimes great sailing can appear where you least expect it—like in the middle of the Colorado Rockies!

"I had just gotten very active in sailing in the southern New Jersey area when my wife finished dental school and landed an oral-surgery residency—and I learned that we'd be shipping off to Denver," began Nick Iwaskow. "As we prepared for the move, I found myself wondering if there would be any sailing in Colorado. Once I arrived and got acclimated, I learned that Denver had a fairly active sailing community, especially for being in the middle of the country. There was fleet racing on Thursdays on Cherry Creek Reservoir, a lot of Laser and Lightning activity. I imagine that most of the people in the Denver sailing community had grown up sailing elsewhere, but nonetheless, they were there now.

"Through the folks I sailed with at Cherry Creek I heard about a place called Dillon Lake. It's about two hours west of Denver, in Summit County. They have an event each year called the Dillon Open, a full-scale regatta with multiple one-design opportunities. A friend I'd made at Cherry Creek wanted me to join him up there. I was hesitant, as I wasn't feeling especially competitive at the time. I told him I'd pencil it in, but that I wasn't completely sold on it. He called a few days later and said, 'I reserved you a Laser and got your entry form in and I'll drive.' I really had no further objections. I guess it was destined to be."

Lake Dillon is a 3,200-acre reservoir that was created in 1963 with the damming of the Blue, Snake, and Ten Mile Rivers. Situated near the resort areas of Keystone and Breckenridge just west of the Continental Divide, the lake rests at an elevation of 9,017 feet, making the Dillon Yacht Club the highest club in America. (Lake Dillon is surrounded by peaks eclipsing 13,000 and 14,000 feet!) The club was established in 1968, at least in part to facilitate the Ski Yachting Championships, a Memorial Day Weekend competition that mixed two days of sailboat races with a day of skiing at nearby Arapahoe Basin. The championships had a short history; in the third year of the race, a fierce mountain thunderstorm swept over the lake, upsetting a number of boats and hospitalizing three sailors. Thereafter, races on Dillon Lake did not begin until June, and skiing was thus removed from the competition. While the Ski Yachting Championships are gone, the Dillon Yacht Club still presides over an active racing program that includes a PHRF fleet, J/24s, J/80s, Ensign 22s, and Santana 22s. The season continues through the end of September, with the Dillon Open (sponsored by Alpine Bank) in early August—which attracts over 150 boats competing in fifteen different one-design classes—being the club's marquee event.

One popular class in the Dillon Open is the Laser, a singlehanded everyman's dinghy that has launched many a competitive sailing career. The Laser was created in 1969 by Bruce Kirby, at the time a newspaper reporter in Montreal. His goal in drawing the Laser was to design a simple, easy-to-rig car-topper boat that would emphasize a *sailor's* ability, rather than the boat's, in competitive situations. To date, over 170,000 Lasers have been built, each one identical in construction. Lasers are now included in Olympic sailing.

Nick made it to the Dillon Open with his friend Steve Davis, and returned a second year before decamping for the East Coast. The memories have stayed with him. "I'll never forget sitting in my boat in the middle of the Rocky Mountains," Nick recalled. "When you grow up sailing in coastal waters, you gain familiarity with small structures. You never imagine you'll be at 9,000 feet, surrounded by 14,000-foot snow-capped peaks. Despite their beauty, the mountains were almost a distraction. You want to take in the majesty of it all, but it takes focus away from your sailing. Conditions were very unlike any coastal venue I've competed, where you have some sort of prevailing wind. On Dillon Lake, the wind was all over the place. You could never count on a consistent, stiff breeze.

"I didn't come in first when I raced at Dillon Lake, nor did I come in last. After the fifth race was completed, I had the sensation that I'd accomplished something. I had sailed at 9,000 feet! Mount Gay Rum sponsored a party after the racing was completed, and there was much bonhomie. I couldn't believe it—here I was in the middle of Colorado, and there was as much enthusiasm for sailboats and racing as you'd find in San Diego or Miami. I didn't expect to find a regatta experience in the middle of the country that could rival coastal events, but I was happily proved wrong. Racing there cured some of my homesickness for the East. It was like I was back home.

"Except for the snowcapped mountains!"

Nick Iwaskow comes from a lineage of sailors—both his parents and grandparents were competitive sailors and commodores of organized yacht clubs in Massachusetts and New Jersey. He has competed at the national level with the Lightning class for over fifteen years, and holds several local, district, and national awards as crew on Lightnings. Nick has also sailed competitively on Lasers and Etchells. When he's not on the water, Nick is a marketing manager at a leading software company.

> **IF YOU GO**

➤ **Getting There:** Lake Dillon is about 90 miles west of the Denver International Airport, which is served by most domestic carriers.

➤ **Best Time to Visit:** The season at this high-altitude lake is late May through late September. Anytime before or after, chances are you could find ice on the lake or snow in the air.

➤ **Charter Operators:** The center for sailing activities on Lake Dillon is the Dillon Yacht Club (970-262-5824; www.dillonyachtclub.com). Some rentals are available from the Dillon Marina (970-468-5100; www.dillonmarina.com).

➤ **On-Shore Accommodations:** Keystone (www.keystoneresort.com) and Breckenridge (breckenridge.snow.com) ski resorts are nearby, and offer many lodgings options.

DESTINATION 12

EASTERN LONG ISLAND SOUND

RECOMMENDED BY **Charlie Olsen** AND **Admiral Robert C. Olsen, Jr.**

Some places are special because once you're there, *you have arrived*. Others can be special because there are *so many places you can go* once you've arrived. The eastern end of Long Island Sound—from the mouth of the Connecticut River east to the Rhode Island border—might fit the latter category.

"Something I love about this part of the Connecticut coast is that there are so many incredible spots easily within reach," Charlie Olsen said. "Block Island, Fishers Island, the eastern stretches of Long Island are all within twenty miles from my home port of Noank. Sail just a bit farther and you can reach Nantucket and Martha's Vineyard. There's great cruising variety here. And the wind is generally quite steady."

"I've sailed to many places in my time," added Charlie's brother, Admiral Robert Olsen. "Up and down the East Coast, Florida, the Caribbean, the Pacific Northwest. Eastern Long Island Sound is still my favorite place to sail. There are so many places that I can go where it's not crowded, because many of these anchoring spots don't have a facilities focus. Many people want to dock and plug in; I like to anchor where it's quiet. Sailing here, you don't have to have a destination imperative, particularly if you're just going out for a couple days. You don't have to sail dawn to dusk to reach a pleasing spot. There are plenty of protected waters, and the bottom tends to be sandy and forgiving."

Options are aplenty along this stretch of Connecticut coast, whether one's seeking a day trip or a cruising weekend. While this area of Connecticut has seen some expansion in recent years due to early retirees and telecommuters recognizing its quality of life (and relative proximity to Manhattan), it's still fairly quiet, especially on weekdays. "The town of Watch Hill [just over the border into Rhode Island] is a very pleasant sail from New

London, though we try to avoid it on the weekends, as it gets a little busy over there," Robert said. "The back side of Watch Hill Point is an especially nice spot to anchor." For Charlie, Fishers Island, just a few miles off the shoreline of New London (though technically part of the state of New York), holds a special appeal. "There's a spot called East Harbor that I like a great deal. The water is very clear. When the sun is behind you at low tide, you can watch the striped bass come out of the eel grass. I could sail by the mansions on Fishers Island a million times and never get tired of it."

Like so much of the New England coastline, eastern Connecticut is rich in maritime lore. The city of New London was a whaling center in the 1800s, third in scope only to New Bedford and Nantucket; displaying a far-sighted awareness of the late-twentieth-century concept of branding, New London proclaimed itself "The Whaling City" (it's unclear whether New London's neighbors to the north took umbrage at this). Just a few miles east of New London rests one of America's most comprehensive maritime museums, Mystic Seaport. It boasts over one million historical nautical photographs, two million maritime artifacts, and nearly five hundred boats, spread over seventeen acres of indoor and outdoor exhibition space. One of the centerpieces of the Mystic collection is the *Charles W. Morgan*, a wooden whaling ship that was launched in New Bedford in 1841. At the time, America boasted more than seven hundred such vessels; today, the *Charles W. Morgan* is the last wooden whaling ship extant.

New London is also the home of the U.S. Coast Guard Academy, which is located along the Thames River and graduates approximately 175 ensigns each year to serve their community and country. (While the U.S. Coast Guard is a segment of the U.S. armed forces, it's unique in that its mission is primarily humanitarian.) Part of the cadets' education involves a stint upon the *Eagle*, which is the largest tall ship that flies the Stars and Stripes (and the only square-rigger in U.S. service). On board the 295-foot *Eagle*, up to 150 students at a given time have the opportunity to exercise the engineering, navigation, and leadership skills they've been honing in the classroom.

When asked what might make an ideal day on the eastern Sound, Robert said, "I'd go wherever the wind takes me, as there are so many options for docking up. It would be nice to get a spinnaker run in, if possible. I like to use different points of the sail if I can. I might go by Fishers or over to Stonington, depending on how crowded it is. If there are lots of boats out, I can easily make the whole loop in a day. I might try to anchor at a spot

13

DESTINATION

where I can get some mussels, and I'll cook them up on my charcoaler. I love to have a swim just before the sun sets. We can take our time getting ready the next morning because we never have that far to go."

Charlie Olsen has been working on boats (specializing in marine carpentry) and racing for forty years. He sails a Cheoy Lee Offshore 40, holds a Coast Guard 50-ton captain's license, and assists in coaching and commissioning for the Coast Guard Academy Sailing Program.

Admiral **Robert C. Olsen, Jr.** is president of Webb Institute, Inc., which focuses exclusively on naval architecture and marine engineering. Before joining Webb, Admiral Olsen served as superintendent of the U.S. Coast Guard Academy in New London, Connecticut. During his thirty-four years of service in the United States Coast Guard, Admiral Olsen served as commanding officer of four Coast Guard cutters and was director of personnel management for the Coast Guard before becoming superintendent.

◀ IF YOU GO ▶

➤ **Getting There:** Eastern Connecticut can be easily accessed from Hartford, which is served by most major carriers.

➤ **Best Time to Visit:** You'll find the best weather in the summer, though early fall conditions are still pleasant, and the crowds have thinned out.

➤ **Charter Operators:** Limited bareboat charters are available from two companies in Mystic: Shanomet Company (484-432-1171; www.shanomet.com) and Sail the Sounds (860-536-5486; www.sailthe sounds.com).

➤ **Moorings:** There are a number of marinas operating on the section of Connecticut coast between New London and Stonington. You'll find a listing of local marinas at www. newlondoncountyguide.com/marinas.

➤ **On-Shore Accommodations:** The towns of New London and Mystic will have the most lodgings options. The area abounds in quaint inns, and you'll find many highlighted at The Bed and Breakfasts of the Mystic Coast (877-699-8579; www.thebbmc.com).

DALMATIAN COAST

RECOMMENDED BY **Jon Wilson**

✳

Many travel-business insiders consider Croatia a hidden gem, combining many of the best aspects of better-known southern European destinations, without the crowds. (Though after Croatia was named "Destination of the Year" by *National Geographic Traveler* in November 2005, this may change!) From a cruising perspective, Jon Wilson has to agree.

"Quite simply, Croatia has it all," he said. "Fantastic crystal-clear water, great sailing conditions, over 1,200 islands and islets to explore, quiet deserted bays and anchorages, and lively cosmopolitan towns steeped in cultural heritage such as Hvar or Korcula."

Croatia has a rich and incredibly complex history, a legacy that's reflected in the conflicts that recently divided Yugoslavia (which was a relatively recent construct in itself, created in its first incarnation in 1918). The turbulence that's dogged Croatia stems largely from its location, at the nexus of central, southern, and eastern Europe, where Latin, Balkan, and Slavic cultures have intermingled. Croatia is across the Adriatic Sea from Italy (the city of Dubrovnik is at the same latitude as Rome) and bordered by Hungary to the north, Slovenia to the northwest, and Montenegro to the southeast; Bosnia and Herzegovina cut into the center of the country, giving Croatia a horseshoe shape.

The Croatian portion of the Dalmatian Coast lies from the border with Montenegro to the island of Rab in the northwest. Whether you work your way north or south, you'll want to linger a few days in the ancient walled city of Dubrovnik. In *Harbors of Enchantment*, author Sylvia Kaul called Dubrovnik "one of the most perfect harbors in the Mediterranean, with golden parapets rising above an indigo sea and a necklace of islands." Most of the damage this medieval city experienced during the Serbian siege of 1991 has been repaired, and in an effort to recognize its historic and cultural significance, the city has been declared a UNESCO World Heritage Site. A walking tour of the two-kilometer

wall that circumscribes the Old Town is a must for visitors; some sections of the wall, first built in the 1200s, are 60 feet thick, and have repelled Venetians, Turks, and Austro-Hungarians over the ages. The city's ancient monasteries also merit a visit. A jaunt to Mount Srd offers a stunning panorama of the city and the sea. Though dating back to medieval times, Dubrovnik has a thoroughly modern vibe, with a thriving café culture and fine restaurants.

The Dalmatian coastline is a study in contrasts, with beaches and steep cliffs alternating with densely wooded islands of cypress and pine, and lemon and orange plantations—a riot of sharp primary colors. Countless coves and bays are part of the coastline's great cruising appeal. Summertime winds in the Adriatic take on three patterns, as writer Les Furnanz points out on www.highonadventure.com: the *mistral*, which blows from the northwest from 12 to 18 knots; the *bora*, a stronger, gustier wind from the northeast; and the *sirocco*, a light wind from the south, associated with the desert (in this case, the Sahara). Most afternoons, you can count on the *mistral* to push you along to your next anchorage.

Though the coastline varies, a strain of commonality in this region of Croatia is the character of the people. "The Croatian people are very friendly and hospitable," Jon continued. "They have a great attitude about life and work—they work hard, enjoy life, treat people well, and are proud of their country and everything it has to offer—which for the outdoor enthusiast is a great deal. In addition to providing some of the best cruising grounds I've encountered, there's excellent wreck diving, spear fishing, sports fishing, white-water rafting, rock climbing, and paragliding."

While the treasures of the 200 miles of Dalmatian Coast in Croatia (and its vaguely unpronounceable names, at least for English tongues) are too many to list here, there are a few stops that should be highlighted. There's Korcula, a walled village dating back to the fifteenth century, and reputedly the birthplace of Marco Polo; Hvar, which is the name of both an island and a town, popular with beach-seeking tourists, and home of the first public theatre in Europe (established in 1612); and Split, with its palm-lined harbor and ruins dating back to Roman times.

Thanks to the prevailing winds and sea currents, the Adriatic along the Dalmatian Coast is clearer and warmer than on the Italian side. These conditions make it quite amenable to swimming, and thanks to a proclivity toward "naturism," bathing suits are quite optional. While written evidence shows that organized nude beaches existed in Croatia as

*OPPOSITE
Croatia is one
of southern
Europe's best-
kept cruising
secrets.*

early as the turn of the last century, officially sanctioned naturism came into being in 1936 when King Edward VIII of England visited the island of Rab and asked Croat authorities for permission to swim nude. Permission was granted, and the famous plunge was taken in the Bay of Kadarola—now known in some circles as English Beach. Nude beaches are especially popular with German and Dutch visitors; this explains why naturist swimming zones are indicated by "FKK" signs (from the German *Freikorperkultur*, or "Free Body Culture").

Jon Wilson is the operations manager for SunSail in Croatia, where the company operates 160 charter yachts. Before landing in Croatia, he worked as a sailing instructor and skipper in Greece, Turkey, the Caribbean, Egypt, and the Maldives. He has sailed extensively throughout the world.

DESTINATION 14

IF YOU GO

➤ **Getting There:** The Croatian capital city of Zagreb is served by many airlines, including Air France, British Airways, and KLM; regular departures are available from Amsterdam, Frankfurt, London, and Paris, among other European cities. From Zagreb, Croatia Airlines (www.croatiaairlines.hr) provides service to either Dubrovnik or Split.

➤ **Best Time to Visit:** The Dalmatian Coast has a Mediterranean climate, with dry, hot summers and cool, misty winters. Most visitors prefer the late spring through early fall.

➤ **Charter Operators:** There are many bareboat charter operators in Croatia, including SunSail (888-350-3568; www.sunsail.com), which has operations in three Croatian locations—Kremik, Kornati, and Dubrovnik.

➤ **On-Shore Accommodations:** The Croatian National Tourist Board (+385 4699 333; www.croatia.hr) lists lodgings options all along the Dalmatian coast.

THE GALÁPAGOS

RECOMMENDED BY **Amy Ullrich**

When an opportunity to take a sailing holiday anywhere in the world presented itself, Amy Ullrich didn't hesitate for long.

"A charter broker I've come to know over my years at *Sail* magazine came to me one day," Amy began, "and asked me, 'What is the one place you'd really like to sail?' I said 'Galápagos' without a moment's hesitation. I'm a longtime fan of Stephen Jay Gould, a wonderful writer on evolution, and I developed an interest in Darwin as a result. I knew I was never going to get there on my own 19-foot boat. My friend was in a position to make it happen. In March of 2006 I flew to Quito, Ecuador, and from there to the islands and *Lammer Law*, a 93-foot sailing trimaran that was, for the next week, home base, transportation, and dive base for me and seven other guests—plus, of course, our guide and a bunch of crew who kept us happy and well fed."

Mention Galápagos, and many images come to mind—giant turtles, sea lions, iguanas, and, of course, the specter of a bearded Charles Darwin, scribbling furiously in a notebook. The first recorded mention of the sixty-one islands that comprise the Galápagos— only thirteen of which are of considerable size—was recorded in 1535 by the bishop of Panama, Tomás de Berlanga. The islands seemed so dry and uninhabitable that he didn't even bother to name them, though he did make note of the "galápago," or giant tortoise, that he encountered there. For the next three hundred years or so, sealers, whalers, and assorted buccaneers used the Galápagos as an occasional base of operations, slaughtering legions of sea turtles for meat. By the time Darwin arrived in 1835, the islands' only permanent human residents were members of a penal colony established by the Ecuadorian government on the island of Floreana.

Darwin had been away from his native England for nearly four years on the *HMS Beagle* by the time he reached the Galápagos, collecting specimens and observations. During the five weeks he spent on the islands, Darwin noted that while the bird and reptile life he encountered on each of the six islands he visited was quite similar, there was some variation in each species. This led him to believe that the animals had adapted over time to the microhabitats of each island. This notion of adaptation or evolution fostered at the Galápagos would be the foundation for *On the Origin of Species*, which would not be published until 1859.

Evolution enthusiasts aside, the great attraction of the Galápagos is the odd and wonderful assemblage of fauna that call the islands home; penguins, finches, pink flamingos, California sea lions, sea turtles, tortoises, fur seals. The eclectic array of animal life on this small archipelago 600 miles off the coast of Ecuador begs the question: How did they get here . . . and why? Scientists believe that the Galápagos were created from volcanic activity on the ocean floor, and that they've never been connected to a continent. All of the resident flora and fauna arrived on the islands by swimming (seals, dolphins, penguins), floating (tortoises, iguanas, insects, some plants), or flying (birds, seeds floating in air currents) from as far afield as the Caribbean and the Antarctic. The "why" is a slightly harder question to answer, though the fact that two important ocean currents—the Southern Humboldt Current and the Northern Panama Current—flow near the Galápagos certainly facilitated and influenced the animals' passage. Once there, they were able to adapt and survive—despite the unbalanced assortment of species—thanks to the absence of predators, with the exception of man.

Over time, special efforts have been made to minimize the footprint mankind leaves on the Galápagos. In 1959—the hundredth anniversary of the publication of Darwin's masterwork—the archipelago was declared a national park; it would later become a UNESCO World Heritage Site. "There are many rules in place, intended to preserve the islands for future generations," Amy observed. "For example, the Park Administration makes a schedule for each passenger vessel, complete with arrival and departure times for morning and afternoon visits; this means you move longer distances during the night. It's part of the effort to equalize the number of people who visit a given island on a given day, and to avoid crowding and overwhelming the animals. The problem is that if you find a place you really enjoy, you can't stay beyond your allotted time. Each island has very well-defined hiking paths; you're not permitted to stray off them. And each group of visitors must

OPPOSITE
A sailboat lets visitors experience all the natural wonders of the Galápagos.

15

DESTINATION

have a government-sanctioned trained guide. But when you think about what the park organization is trying to do—protect this living museum of animals, as well as the islands themselves, *and* make them accessible to visitors—the regulations seem reasonable."

While it is possible to sail to the Galápagos on your own boat—provided you retain a guide upon your arrival—most visitors arrive by plane and stay for a week. "The majority of visitors are on cruise ships, though there is a variety of charter boats, both power and sail," Amy said. "I like the atmosphere of a 'real' boat like *Lammer Law*, and since I'm a sailor by vocation as well as avocation, I appreciate the ability to sail when there's enough wind. Though our emphasis was on our two daily hikes, snorkeling, diving, talks by the guide, and numerous meals, we did get in some sailing.

"On a typical day, our group would rise before dawn so we could be on shore at sunrise; this is an ideal time for photographers, and there's plenty to keep you busy with your camera. It does get hot in the middle of the day, so it's wise to take advantage of the cooler mornings and late afternoons.

"Even though I'd read in many guidebooks—my pretrip prep—how close you can get to the animals (without touching, of course), I was unprepared for the reality of being nose to nose with a frigate bird or a sea lion. You can sneak up pretty close to the giant Galápagos tortoises if you visit the preserve on Santa Cruz Island, but they roar if you get *too* close.

"While coral doesn't grow in the cold waters around the Galápagos, there's no shortage of colorful fish, as well as sharks and rays. Many of the beaches are full of female sea lions and their pups, and it was a rare snorkel that didn't include a meeting with some of them. The divers—and how I wished I had been among them—had a nice meeting with a school of hammerhead sharks. At some point in the day, between the morning snack and afternoon tea, we'd eat lunch and then move to our next anchorage. Then there would be another hike or two. Every day was so wonderful and different."

One of the fascinating creatures you'll see at the Galápagos is the blue-footed boobie, known for its cross-eyed visage and eccentric mating dance; one explanation for its name is that Spanish visitors, upon seeing the birds, called them *bobos* (clowns). Nature writer Michelle Alten described the dance this way in the January/February 1998 issue of *International Wildlife*:

. . . [T]he male goose-steps to attract a female's attention. A female, accepting the male's ostentatious invitation, patters over. The birds, a couple of yards away from other ground-nesting blue-foots, flash their bright turquoise webbed feet and point their tails skyward. For a moment, the birds pause and turn away from each other, casting a timid glance in the opposite direction. Then the male reaches for a pebble, placing it on an imaginary nest. The female blue-foot offers a branch, and the two gently tap bills.

"We came upon a group of blue-footed boobies doing their mating dances," Amy recalled. "Their feet are so very blue. It's stayed with me."

Amy Ullrich is managing editor of *Sail* magazine and responsible for the magazine's coverage of chartering. She is happy to volunteer for assignments.

IF YOU GO

➤ **Getting There:** Visitors generally fly to the Ecuadorian capital of Quito, and from there fly to the Galápagos. Quito is served from Miami by LAN Ecuador, Continental, Delta, and American Airlines, among others. TAME (www.tame.com.ec) offers flights to San Cristóbal.

➤ **Best Time to Visit:** December to May, as weather is warm and winds are light.

➤ **Charter Operators:** A number of groups lead sailboat trips to the Galápagos, including Oceanic Society (800-326-7491; www.oceanic-society.org), the group that Amy Ullrich traveled with.

➤ **Moorings:** Visiting boats may only moor in designated locations to protect the region's sensitive ecosystem, and moorings are limited. It's not recommended that you travel to the Galápagos without having first reserved mooring space of some sort. Port services are available on the islands of Isabela, San Cristóbal, and Santa Cruz.

➤ **On-Shore Accommodations:** Galápagos Safari Camp (www.galapagossafaricamp.com) is a newly opened eco-lodge on the island of Santa Cruz. Discover Galápagos (www.discovergalapagos.com) provides a list of hotels in Quito.

15

DESTINATION

BISCAYNE BAY

RECOMMENDED BY **Sean Ferrell**

✳

For better or worse, the television program *Miami Vice* (and its subsequent film remake) has given many non-Floridians their most vivid picture of southeastern Florida's largest city and its neighbor, Miami Beach. Miamians will tell you that the show certainly got many things wrong. But one aspect of the region that was well captured is its colors—both in the pastel shades of actor Don Johnson's clothing and in the shades of the water of Biscayne Bay.

"The water is a beautiful turquoise," said Sean Ferrell, "and it's always warm. Whether you're racing or cruising, the waters of Biscayne Bay have a very calming effect."

Biscayne Bay is roughly 35 miles long and up to 8 miles wide, and runs south from the city of Miami down to Key Largo. Most of the bay is buffered on the east by a series of manmade and natural islands, including Key Biscayne, Elliot Key, and the Scattered Keys. "The islands on the east side keep the waves and the rough weather out," Sean added. Biscayne Bay opens to the Atlantic at a spot called the Safety Valves, and to Florida Bay between Key Largo and the mainland. Much of the bay rests within the boundaries of Biscayne National Park.

Miami and adjacent Miami Beach began to come of age in the 1920s, fostered by legalized gambling and a relaxed attitude toward Prohibition. With the crowds of northerners who arrived to enjoy the warmth—and perhaps, the vice—came the development of the South Florida Boat Racing Association. Informal race planning meetings were held at various spots along the waterfront, and early races were conducted off Point View (a.k.a. Millionaire's Row). The cobbled-together association scored several coups in its early years, first organizing the Sir Thomas Lipton Cup Race (named for the tea magnate) off Miami, then the Miami-Nassau Race. By the end of 1934, the South Florida Boat Racing

OPPOSITE

Biscayne Bay offers the excitement of Miami and the solitude of the northern Keys within an easy day's sail.

16

DESTINATION

Association had changed its name to the Miami Yacht Club; the name is said to have been taken from a nightclub north of the Royal Palm Yacht Basin.

Today the club operates from an ideal spot on Watson Island, just east of downtown Miami. Though their docks and piers were destroyed by Hurricane Andrew in 1992, facilities have been successfully rebuilt, allowing the club to continue to sponsor a number of races. One local favorite is the Miami–Key Largo Race, which occurs each year toward the end of April. "It's a single-start race, with cats on one line, monohulls on the other," Sean said. "The race is forty-three miles. Everyone stays down overnight, and there's quite a party. The next day, everyone sails back, though at a slightly more relaxed pace. We had over two hundred boats participating last year. The course record is one hour and forty-six minutes—the wind was blowing at almost thirty knots!" The race has been held since 1955, and all proceeds go to support the club's youth sailing programs.

Miami and Biscayne Bay are also home to the Acura Miami Race Week, a dual-venue event with ocean divisions and bay divisions.

One event that Miami sailors are especially proud of is the Rolex Miami Olympic Classes Regatta (OCR). "It's an Olympics qualifying event, one of only five in the world," Sean continued. "People come from all over—more than six hundred of the most talented sailors in the world." Sailors compete in thirteen Olympic and Paralympic classes. Paralympic sailing is a fairly recent arrival on the competitive circuit. The U.S. Disabled Sailing Team was formed in 1998, and sent its first team to the Paralympics in Sydney in 2000, where paralympic sailing debuted as a full-medal sport. Racers compete in three classes—Individual (2.4mR), Double Team (SKUD-18), and Triple Team (Sonar). Events are open to visually impaired people and people with disabilities affecting movement or balance. For the Triple Team events, each crew member is classified on a scale of 1 to 7 based upon their degree of disability (with one indicating greatest disability); total crew points cannot exceed fourteen. Jennifer French sailed actively on the competitive circuit before a snowboarding accident left her a quadriplegic in 1998. She continues to sail competitively today. "A compelling aspect of sailing is that it's not a separate sport, like wheelchair basketball or rugby; there's a wide range of disabilities participating," Jennifer said. "Once you've set your wheelchair or crutches on the dock and are out on the water, there are no handicaps; it's whoever crosses the finish line first. I compete in many events that include both able-bodied and disabled sailors. There's no sympathy on the race course. And that's just how I like it."

As mentioned above, most of Biscayne Bay rests within the confines of Biscayne National Park, the largest marine park in the national park system, with 95 percent of its 207 square miles covered by water. The park is home to Florida's longest stretch of intact mangrove forest, and over two hundred species of fish. It also includes some forty islands of the Florida keys that are often overlooked, as they rest north of Key Largo, where the bridge from the mainland connects. These keys, which can only be reached by boat, give a sense of what south Florida was like before the developers so convincingly portrayed in the works of Carl Hiaasen descended upon the coast. "You can set off for a day sail from Miami on a Saturday morning and get to the bottom of Biscayne Bay by early afternoon. The snorkeling is fantastic in the park waters—they're quite famous for that. Many times we go down with the intention of coming back in the late afternoon. However, it's so pleasant, we often decide to stay overnight and return on Sunday."

Sean Ferrell is a past commodore of the Miami Yacht Club, and has been racing sailboats for many years. He is a US Sailing certified race officer, and has participated in a multitude of regattas, including both multihulls and monohulls. His multihull regatta experience includes the Key Largo Race, The Steeplechase, the Hobie Wave Nationals, the Tornado Nationals, and many Olympic Class regattas. Sean is a research associate with the Miami Project to Cure Paralysis, at the University of Miami School of Medicine.

▶ IF YOU GO ◀

➤ **Getting There:** Biscayne Bay laps at the shoreline of Miami, which is served by most major air carriers.

➤ **Best Time to Visit:** Miami is conducive to sailing year round, though the winter months are slightly cooler and less humid.

➤ **Charter Operators:** Operators include Florida Yacht Charters & Sales (800-537-0050; www.floridayacht.com) and Go Island Hop (800-island-hop; www.goislandhop.com).

➤ **Moorings:** Berths are generally available at Miami Beach Marina (305-673-6000; www.miamibeachmarina.com).

➤ **On-Shore Accommodations:** The Miami Beach Chamber of Commerce (305-672-1270; www.miamibeachchamber.com) has extensive accommodations listings.

16

DESTINATION

KEY WEST

RECOMMENDED BY **Brian Bissell**

✳

When a big regatta comes to town, the town in question has an opportunity to shine. During race week, perhaps no town shines like Key West, as Brian Bissell happily recalls.

"I first sailed at Key West during Race Week in 2003, crewing on a boat that was racing in the PHRF class. Key West is a pretty lively place all the time. But when you have three hundred sailboats, crew, and other assorted supporters and spectators descend on the place, it has an incredible vibe. It doesn't hurt that the race, which is generally scheduled for January, gives the many competitors who have been in snow and cold for a while a chance to enjoy a great break from the weather. The turquoise blue of the water is a wonderful contrast to the bleak gray that marks many winter days in the Northeast."

While technically part of Florida and the United States, Key West has always stood somewhat apart, dancing to the beat of its own bohemian drum. Claimed at various times by Spain, England, and several private citizens, the early settlers of Key West—mostly Bahamians and Anglos from the recently created United States—claimed no great allegiance to any nation beyond Duval Street. Situated at the southern tip of the continental United States, Key West is strategically perched above the Florida Straits, a popular commercial shipping lane where the Gulf Stream begins making its way east. (Several markers on Key West claim to be the most southerly point in the U.S.; maps show that point to be a privately owned island named Ballast.) Given this, and the islanders' somewhat opportunistic bent, it's not surprising that for a time in the nineteenth century, residents made a fine living by scavenging the remains of sunken ships.

If leery of outside interference, Key West has always been welcoming to outsiders, from both different geographic and different social circles. Gays found acceptance here, as did artists; it's almost impossible to throw a stone in Old Town and not hit a Hemingway

OPPOSITE
Key West Race Week in January provides a jolt of warm-weather excitement for snowbound racers.

placard of one sort or another, and the playwright Tennessee Williams called Key West home for the later years of his life. The tropical, off-the-grid ambiance of Key West has helped fuel a lively nightlife. "Duval Street has a lot of fun restaurants and bars," Brian went on, "and you get the sense that most of the people down here are out to have a good time. It's hard to beat a plate of conch fritters and a mudslide." For visitors, evening reveling is usually preceded by a trip to the Mallory Dock to take in the Sunset Celebration, where buskers and hustlers beckon the sun into the Gulf of Mexico.

Whether it's the northern soul's need for winter sunshine or the lure of Key West's rich off-the-water attractions, Key West Race Week has emerged as one of the foremost regattas in the U.S. Entries from thirty states and twenty countries make the trek south; these entries include boats in twenty classes, which compete in four divisions. For the seven days of the event, the sailing community takes over Old Town Key West; the goings-on in the "Race Village" rival the hijinks of the sunsetters on Mallory Dock. "Each year, the race sponsors have a circus tent set up that can accommodate the entire regatta—four thousand people!" Brian continued. "One of the sponsors is Mount Gay Rum, and as you might guess, there are free rum drinks. There's a huge video screen center stage in the tent where they play footage of the day. Likewise, there are daily awards for the best performances." The conditions don't disappoint either. The winter winds are generally very steady; during the 2006 Race Week sailors had winds of at least 11 knots to work with each of the five days of racing, with winds reaching 20 to 30 knots on several days.

Brian Bissell has competed in three Key West Race Weeks, but the 2006 regatta was especially sweet, as he and his crew won their class, the Mumm 30. "Sailing a Mumm 30, the weight of your crew is significant," Brian explained. "You want to be near the maximum weight the boat can handle so you have the ballast you need to counteract the pressure of the wind on the sail. But you can't be over. When our guys arrived, we were seventeen pounds over. We had twelve hours to get our weight down. We jogged, sat in our van with the heat on, anything to get that weight off. We made it with fourteen pounds to spare. Once we got on the water, the racing was pretty hairy, as the winds were especially strong for a few days. We had broken masts, wipeouts. Very exciting.

"The last race of the week stands out in particular for me—it was a case of the slow and steady boat winning the race. It was one of those big-wind days, and the boats were making the turn to come back in toward the finish line. Now on a Mumm 30, you have a choice of two spinnakers—a masthead kite and a fractional. The bigger kite propels you faster, but it's also tougher to handle. We opted to go with the smaller kite, but all of our competitors went with the big sail . . . and promptly blew past us. There was a spot in the course not too far from the finish when you had to jibe. When the boats with the big kites went to jibe, they all capsized—every last one. We breezed in to victory.

"That night at the party in the Big Tent, they were showing films on the video screen of the other boats capsizing. When we went up to get our awards, there was a close-up of our boat—*TeamBOLD*—crossing the finishing line."

Brian Bissell works for North Sails One-Design Team out of Annapolis, Maryland. He has been competitively racing since he was five years old. He won numerous junior sailing championships including three ISSA (High School) National Championships. He was a three-time All-American at Georgetown University. At Georgetown he finished first, second, and third at the ICSA (College) North Americans. In the J/24 he has won the U.S. National, North American, and World Championships. A tactician, main trimmer, and crew manager on board the Mumm 30, he won the 2005 North American, 2006 Key West Race Week, and 2006 North American circuit. Brian placed third in the 2006 Snipe North Americans, qualifying him to sail in the Snipe World Championships in 2007.

◄ IF YOU GO ►

➤ **Getting There:** Most visitors will fly to Miami, which is served by most major air carriers. From there, it's about a 150-mile drive to Key West.

➤ **Best Time to Visit:** If you're looking for extra excitement, Key West Race Week is traditionally held in late January. Conditions are conducive to sailing year round.

➤ **Charter Operators:** Southernmost Sailing (305-293-1883; www.southernmostsailing. com) offers bareboat charters; several other outfitters offer skippered day cruises.

➤ **Moorings:** A number of marinas serve Key West, including Key West Yacht Club Marina (305-296-3446) and Oceanside Marina (305-294-4676).

➤ **On-Shore Accommodations:** The Key West Florida Official Tourism Web site (www. fla-keys.com/keywest) has extensive accommodations listings.

France

HYÈRES

RECOMMENDED BY **Lawrence White**

✴

Mention France and sailing in the same breath, and it's likely that the French Riviera springs to mind: an anchorage off the coast of Cannes, perhaps, from which you might don formal wear and dinghy into port to view a starlet-sprinkled film premiere.

If you're a serious racer, however, your thoughts might drift a bit to the south and west, to the city of Hyères. "I spent several seasons as a judge at pre-Olympic regattas in Hyères," said Lawrence White, "and found the area very attractive. There's a lovely bay with excellent facilities for recreational sailing, and the off-lying islands—Iles d'Or, or Golden Islands—both are beautiful and provide shelter from the open sea."

The city of Hyères is the southernmost municipality in the Provence region of France, jutting out into the Mediterranean at the foot of the Maures Hills. The old town of Hyères, which features the Tower of Saint-Blaise (which dates back to the twelfth century and was once occupied by the Knights Templar), is set back from the water and reflects the character of an old Provence village; the waterside areas, though lacking in Old World ambiance, are geared very much to the sailing community. While dating back to medieval times, Hyères gained prominence in the 1700s for its mild climate, which made it an ideal place to grow exotic trees, such as its trademark palm. In the nineteenth century, the city became a winter retreat for those who could afford to flee the cold of northern Europe; many writers of the late Victorian period, including Leo Tolstoy and Joseph Conrad, found inspiration—or at least sunshine—in Hyères. With the coastal frontage east of town and the Presqu'ile de Giens peninsula, which stretches south, Hyères boasts over 27 miles of coastline, and more than 100 square miles of ideal sailing grounds, with Hyères Bay (east of the peninsula) the focal point of the action. Porquerolles, the largest of the Golden Isles, is home to three vineyards and a large park.

OPPOSITE
Hyères is the
site of a major
International
Sailing
Federation
event, the
Semaine
Olympique
Française.

DESTINATION 18

85

Though cruisers will find worthy attractions around Hyères, racers come here with their sights set on a larger goal—a chance to participate in the Olympics.

Sailing has been part of the modern Olympic Games almost since their inception, though when it premiered in 1900, the sport was known as "yachting"; the term "sailing" was not used until 2000. The first regatta took place on the Seine near Paris and included seven classes—an "open class," and then six other classes based upon weight. Forty-two boats competed in that Olympic event, many of them from France (as there were no limits on the number of entries per nation). By 1908, classes were established based on boat length—6, 7, 8, 12, and 15 meters. While women occasionally crewed on Olympic boats, there were no female-only disciplines until 1988 in Korea, when the Women's Double-handed Dinghy (470) race was launched (and won by Americans Allison Jolley and Lynne Jewell). In the 2004 Olympics in Athens, four hundred sailors representing sixty-one nations raced in eleven one-design events: Men's Singlehanded Dinghy (Finn), Women's Singlehanded Dinghy (Europe), Men's Doublehanded Dinghy (470), Women's Double-handed Dinghy (470), Open Doublehanded High-Performance Dinghy (49er), Open Singlehanded Dinghy (Laser), Men's Doublehanded Keelboat (Star), Open Doublehanded Multihull (Tornado), Women's Triplehanded Keelboat (Yngling), and men's and women's windsurfing.

As an International Sailing Federation (ISAF, formerly IYRU) Grade 1 event, the Semaine Olympique Française (SOF) in Hyères is a key stop on an international circuit that helps determine which sailors will participate in ISAF World Sailing Games and, ultimately, the next Olympics. The event is held the last week of April each year; in 2006, it attracted more than a thousand sailors from fifty countries. "People interested in Olympic racing begin working their way along the Mediterranean coast in February," Larry explained. "The first few events are in Spain. At the event in Hyères, ten or twelve judges come from different countries. Some are on the water to enforce rules, others oversee hearings when a protest arises. From a judging perspective, a sensitive issue as of late has been whether or not to enforce rules on the water—like a referee in a football game. The trend is in this direction, with judges on the water more and more, imposing penalties when they occur. This goes against the basic self-policing premise in sailing. After all, it's written in the rules that you agree to follow the rules. Some of us who have a few miles on us have a concern about this trend."

Lawrence White was a vice president of US Sailing and served twice on its Executive Committee. An active competitor in many classes and offshore, Larry has also diligently served the amateur racing community. He started college racing in 1943 at MIT; after graduating from MIT he attended the U.S. Coast Guard Academy, graduating in 1951, and served in the Coast Guard until 1979, when he retired as a captain (O-6). In the years since, he has worked with sailors and in the sport as a volunteer. In 1980 he was elected to the ICYRA Hall of Fame and the Coast Guard Academy's Athletic Hall of Fame. Returning to college sailing, Larry was involved in several capacities including judging, and in 1986 revived Afterguard, the then-ICYRA alumni association. A fiftieth anniversary regatta drew luminaries including Ted Turner and Gary Jobson. In that same year Larry also accepted the challenge to reinvigorate the Coast Guard Academy's sailing program. From 1989 to 2005, Larry served as president of the Interscholastic Yacht Racing Association (now known as the Interscholastic Sailing Association). He has served as a U.S. judge and an international judge for twenty years. Larry was recently awarded the US Sailing Herreshoff Trophy for his outstanding contributions to the development of the sport and the Intercollegiate Sailing Association's Lifetime Achievment Award. He now enjoys watching his grandson Andrew grow and develop in his love of sailing.

IF YOU GO

➤ **Getting There:** Many international visitors will fly to Paris and then on to Toulon-Hyères Airport, which is served by Air France.

➤ **Best Time to Visit:** Hyères enjoys a pleasant Mediterranean climate year round. For racing enthusiasts, late April is the time to be in Hyères.

➤ **Charter Operators:** CharterWorld.com (www.charterworld.com) offers both bareboat and crewed yachts.

➤ **Moorings:** Moorings can be found at Le Neil (+33 494 582149), Port Les Salettes (+33 494 585625), and Port de Plaisance St-Pierre (+33 494 125440).

➤ **On-Shore Accommodations:** The Hyères Office of Tourism (+33 494 018451; www.ot-hyères.fr) has extensive accommodations listings.

MOPELIA

RECOMMENDED BY **John Neal**

✴

Few sailors have heard of the small island of Mopelia (also known as Maupihau), and fewer still have anchored in its seldom-visited lagoon. If he finds himself in the region, adventurer/educator John Neal makes it a point to anchor. "We've made some friends ashore over the years," John said, "and each time we stop, we have a big potluck dinner on the beach. There's not much in the way of entertainment going on on Mopelia; I think the people working there are eager for a chance to socialize."

Mopelia is situated about 150 miles west of Bora Bora (an overnight sail if winds are cooperative) and might qualify as the quintessential tropical island, unburnished by Club Med–like visions of what a tropical island should be. Much of Mopelia is given over to coconut trees, remnants of a plantation that was established on the island at the turn of the last century. There are a few abandoned cement houses and two thatched houses on stilts that rest near the lagoon. These dwellings have periodically provided shelter for workers who harvest copra (dried coconut) from the coconut plantation and pearl shells from the lagoon, where they are cultivated. Islanders have also periodically used Mopelia as a rearing ground for sea turtles, captured from the nearby Scilly Islands; the endangered turtles are ultimately smuggled to Tahiti. This practice is illegal, but provides a great economic boon to the island's few residents, who have long eaten turtle meat as part of their culture. "There's no radio transmitter on the island," John added, "really little of anything but coconut trees and the coral. Of the 350 to 400 boats a year that are crossing the Pacific in the vicinity of Mopelia, I would guess that ten boats stop."

Mopelia is the Society Islands' only atoll (a low coral island consisting of reef surrounding a central depression) that has a navigable pass into the lagoon—though the pass is *barely* navigable, which certainly limits the island's number of visitors. "Many times

OPPOSITE
Once you pass into Mopelia's lagoon, you've entered your own tropical paradise.

DESTINATION 19

when we've visited Mopelia, the sluice has been unpassable," John recalled. "It's very narrow, there's sharp coral on either side, and the current running against you can be 9 knots. On those occasions, we've anchored outside the pass and taken a rubber boat in to explore. Still, there have been times when the current is with us and we've been able to get through with little difficulty. Once you're inside, the lagoon is beautiful, like a lake, though there are coral patches and pearl-farm floats that you need to be conscious of."

One of Mopelia's most colorful visitors in the last century was a self-styled German pirate/aristocrat named Count Felix von Luckner. John related the tale of the count's first and last trip to Mopelia: "During the early years of World War I, von Luckner disguised his heavily armed sailing ship, the *Seeadler*, as a merchant vessel and sank fifteen Allied ships, mostly unarmed trading schooners. A gentleman as well as a pirate, von Luckner treated his captives well after stripping their schooners of useful supplies; a tale goes that after a French ship carrying Champagne was sunk, crew and captives shared in the bubbly and quite a party was had! In the summer of 1916, von Luckner and the *Seeadler* anchored outside Mopelia's lagoon and made landing to stock up on provisions. He and his men were greeted by islanders, who were then working the coconut plantation, with a fabulous feast of roast pork, lobster, turtle soup, and sea-bird omelets. While the crew was taking on water and foodstuffs, a squall blew through, splintering the *Seeadler* on the reef, and sending its cargo—which was rumored to include significant quantities of gold—to the bottom. The count eventually transformed the *Seeadler*'s eighteen-foot motor launch into a gaff-rigged motorsailer and set sail with a portion of his crew to capture a new sailing ship and return to his looting ways. He made it as far as Fiji before being captured and held as a prisoner of war. Count von Luckner never returned to Mopelia to retrieve the alleged treasure. This leads me to believe that the treasure wasn't off Mopelia after all!"

Treasure or not, an hour spent snorkeling around the wreck of the *Seeadler* is part of the Mopelia experience. "The wreck is right near the pass into the lagoon, and there are often sharks hanging out there, waiting to intercept baitfish that get sucked in and out with the tide," John continued. "They're no bother to us, though. While we've yet to uncover any gold, we have come across three huge anchors, a windlass, a rudder, an air tank, tons of corroded pipes, and brass shell casings."

John has many happy memories of feasts he's enjoyed with Mopelian residents and passing voyagers. "On one occasion, we ventured out beyond the reef to trap lobster. My wife at the time and I weren't very adept at catching them, but our Mopelian friends caught fifteen and we enjoyed quite a party. On my most recent trip, we were joined by members of several other boats that happened to be in the area, including a French family and an Australian group. We set up an amazing bonfire on the beach and each group contributed food from their holds; one of our local friends, named Kaloni, brought two huge cooked coconut crabs. Under the moon and stars and coconut trees upon a white sand beach that glowed in the moonlight, we had thirty people of many nationalities talking and laughing and singing songs in French, English and Tahitian."

John Neal's ocean-sailing background dates to 1974 when he sailed 15,000 miles through the South Pacific, part of the time single-handed on his 27-foot Vega sloop. His book chronicling that adventure, *Log of the* Mahina, *a Tale of the South Pacific,* became a bestseller. John also coauthored *Mahina Tiare, Pacific Passages*, which was published in 1993. John has more than 240,000 miles of sailing experience, ranging from Norway to Alaska to Antarctica, but his passion is teaching ocean cruising. John and his wife, Amanda, now operate Mahina Expeditions (360-378-6131; www.mahina.com), which helps prepare highly motivated sailors to conduct long-range offshore sailing expeditions. Since 1976, John has conducted over 125 weekend offshore cruising seminars for people considering long-distance ocean cruising on their own sailboats.

IF YOU GO

➤ **Getting There:** To reach Mopelia, you'll first need to reach Bora Bora to charter a boat. To reach Bora Bora, you'll first need to reach Tahiti-Nui in French Polynesia. The Tahiti-Faa'a International Airport is served by a number of carriers, including Hawaiian, Air France, Air New Zealand, and Qantas. From Tahiti, several air charter services offer scheduled flights to Bora Bora, including Air Tahiti.

➤ **Best Time to Visit:** May through October—this is Mopelia's dry season. Temperatures hover in the high seventies.

➤ **Charter Operators:** Bora Bora offers many charter operators providing both skippered and bareboat charters (most are actually situated on the nearby island Raiatea). A comprehensive list is found at www.boraboraisland.com/sailing.html#sail.

➤ **On-Shore Accommodations:** The Bora Bora Island Web site (www.boraboraisland.com) gathers a range of accommodations in Bora Bora.

DODECANESE ISLANDS

RECOMMENDED BY **Diane Edwards**

When Americans conjure up an image of Mediterranean indolence, it is often the Greek Isles that come to mind. The macropicture involves tidy whitewashed villages that stand out in startling relief from vibrant blue seas and skies; the micropicture might include a plate of grape leaves and a shot glass of ouzo. Truth be told, the mental canvas is not that different from the decorative prints one might find in a Greek diner.

By most reports, it's better in person.

"Since I come from England, Greece did not originally have the exotic appeal for me that it does for many American visitors," Diane Edwards began. "Many Brits see Greece as one more package-tour destination—a three-hour plane ride to the sunshine. I spent a season there working on a sailboat, and fell in love with the place—though I still thought there must be something better elsewhere. I spent time in the Caribbean, which was the 'Wow' place for British sailors, and did enough boat-bumming to see many of the world's famous sailing destinations. But when I decided to start up my own charter biz, Greece drew me back: the outgoing, friendly nature of the people; the fantastic *taverna* culture, which is so perfect for cruising sailors; the exciting but very rarely dangerous wind conditions; the variety of islands all within such easy reach of each other. There are places with more natural beauty and with equally reliable sailing conditions, but they seem very homogenized next to the Greek Isles, each of which has its own idiosyncratic character. All these facets added up to make Greece a superb location to give people a two-week taste of the cruising life."

Put another way, if it was good enough for Odysseus, it will probably be good enough for you!

OPPOSITE

If you avoid the islands whose names you recognize, you'll increase your odds of finding the "real" Greece.

The Dodecanese Islands, in the easternmost region of Greece in the Aegean Sea, are a favorite cruising ground for Diane, for both their cultural diversity and lack of crowds. The name translates from the Greek as "twelve islands," though in reality the complex comprises a total of 163 islands and islets, twenty-six of which are populated—and twelve of which are considered to be "major" islands: Rhodes, Kos, Astipalea, Kalimnos, Karpathos, Kassos, Kastelorizo, Leros, Nissiros, Patmos, Simi, and Tilos. Of the Dodecanese, Rhodes is certainly the best known, recognized for its archeological sites that date back three thousand years; one such site is the Acropolis (high city) of Lindos, which dates back to 1100 B.C. and includes the Doric temple of Athena. Those venturing to Rhodes to take in the Colossus, immortalized as one of the Seven Wonders of the World, will be greatly disappointed. The statue was created between 292 B.C. and 280 B.C. from stone, marble, and bronze, and is believed to have stood 110 feet tall; a likeness of the god Helios, it was commissioned to celebrate the successful defense of Rhodes from Demetrius, a great besieger of cities at the time. The statue was destroyed by an earthquake only fifty-six years after its completion; visitors continued to come to Rhodes to marvel at the remains for eight centuries, until the remnants were sold to a traveling salesman by occupying Arab forces. These remnants were broken down and sold as souvenirs.

Unless you're in search of souvenirs, Diane would recommend that you minimize your stay on the better-known islands. "The islands have changed a lot in the past twenty years," she observed. "Sadly, most of the better-known ones are hardly recognizable as 'Greece' these days. On some you'll find McDonald's, Irish bars, and English breakfasts; if this is what you want, choose places like Rhodes, which have been sanitized to prevent any culture shock. If you're looking for the 'real Greece,' get out your charts and stick the pin in the most obscure-looking island you can find!"

What will you find on these lesser-known islands? Most will have their share of archeological treasures—especially fortresses, monasteries, and castles from the islands' Byzantine past. There will be secluded white beaches, crystal-clear blue coves, and sun-baked hillsides to explore. And whenever you stumble upon a small fishing village, there will be a church, a few dozen goats, and a welcoming *taverna*—and inevitably warm encounters with the always friendly Greek people. (*Taverna*s, by the way, are not taverns, but casual family-oriented restaurants, though ouzo, beer, and wine are available.) "On the little islands, the old traditional values of hospitality still hold true, and some of the best parties we've ever had have been at a local islander's home," Diane continued. "Often when one of our Greek buddies gets into a festive mood (something it seems that all Greeks are genetically predisposed to do), we'll be there, dancing till three a.m. under the stars."

One of the best pieces of advice Diane can offer new island cruisers is to abandon their conventional notions of time. "Greece—especially the islands—gives visitors the sense that they are exploring a *very* foreign land, not a charter member of the European Union," Diane added. "The general environment tends to be totally disorganized, chaotic, laid back—we say that people here operate on 'GMT'—Greek Maybe Time. Running a business here, we'd often give our left arm for some 'first-world' organization and efficiency. But from the point of view of visitors, it's a total contrast to the city lifestyle at home. If visitors can't leave their Westernized notions of timekeeping behind, GMT will drive them potty. If they can get into 'Greek Mode,' they'll find that they've forgotten how to get uptight!"

Diane Edwards is the owner of SeaScape (www.seascape-sail.com), which leads charter sailing trips throughout Greece, Turkey, and Thailand. A native of England, Diane vacillated between boat-bumming and the software industry before taking the plunge with her first boat in Greece, *Vassilis.*

IF YOU GO

➤ **Getting There:** Many international visitors will fly to Athens and then on to the islands of Kos or Rhodes, where many charter companies operate. Service from Athens is available on Olympic Airlines and Aegean Airlines.

➤ **Best Time to Visit:** The height of the sailing season is late April to early October, with meltemi winds most consistent in July and August.

➤ **Charter Operators:** SeaScape (877-273-2722; www.seascape-sail.com) offers skippered cruises throughout the Dodecanese. Many outfits offer bareboat charters in the Aegean, including The Moorings (888-952-8420; www.moorings.com).

➤ **On-Shore Accommodations:** The Hellenic Chamber of Hotels (+30 210 331 0022; www.grhotels.gr) is a good starting point for on-shore accommodations in Greece.

20

DESTINATION

LAHAINA TO HONOLULU

RECOMMENDED BY **Mike Rothwell**

✳

By pedigree, Mike Rothwell was destined to sail the waters off Hawaii. "My great-great-grandfather jumped off the well-known New Bedford–based whaler *Charles W. Morgan* on the big island of Hawaii," Mike said. "He sailed around the world twice as a boat steerer and harpooner. I've been sailing here—and racing—as long as I can remember."

Conduct an Internet search for "regatta" and "Hawaii," and you're as likely to come up with search results for canoe races as sailboat races. Until Captain Cook arrived in 1778, canoes *were* the boats of Hawaii, and today they still grab much of the popular boating public's mindshare. With their towering volcanoes, lush tropical rainforests, and pristine beaches, the islands of Hawaii make up an incomparable Pacific idyll. Yet it can be an idyll that presents challenges for the less seasoned cruiser, as the water can be rough and the sheltered anchorages few and far between. Still, the islands (particularly Oahu) are an essential stopping point for sailors crossing the Pacific, and the home of several noteworthy races. These include the Waikiki Offshore Series (an offshoot of the Kenwood Cup Hawaii International Offshore Series, sponsored by the Waikiki Yacht Club) and the Lipton Cup (sponsored by the Hawaii Yacht Racing Association). Two other open ocean races conclude here as well: the TransPac (which goes from Los Angeles to Honolulu and runs each odd-numbered year) and the Victoria (British Columbia) to Maui Race (held each even numbered year), which ends at the Lahaina Yacht Club.

The local race that's closest to Mike's heart—and perhaps most representative of the laid-back Hawaii racing experience—is the Lahaina to Honolulu Return Regatta. "From the time I was a boy, my dad used to take me along on this race," Mike recalled. "It's always held on Labor Day. There were occasions when there was little or no wind, and we

OPPOSITE
The Lahaina
to Honolulu
Return Regatta
captures
the laid-back
Hawaiian
attitude toward
racing.

wouldn't get back until four a.m. School started the next day, and I thought our late arrival would be a sure-fire ticket to skipping school, but my dad always said, 'No way!'"

The one-day race is, on some levels, a great excuse for a little vacation and a party. "When I compete, I tend to take some time off so we can take our time on the way over to Maui," Mike explained. "Hawaii doesn't have the number of sheltered anchorages that you'll find in many places, but there are still some fun little places to pop in and anchor. One spot I like very much is Manele Bay, on the back side of the island of Lanai. There's a resort there owned by Four Seasons; it's the place where Bill Gates was married, back in 1994. You can anchor in a harbor there and walk over to the resort." Unless, of course, the Gateses are visiting. During the time of the ceremony, Gates rented every hotel room at the hotel—250 rooms—and is said to have chartered every available helicopter in the area, all to ensure his nuptials a modicum of privacy. The fifteen-minute ceremony was con- ducted on the twelfth tee of the resort's golf course overlooking Hulopoe Bay; the price tag for the wedding was one million dollars.

"From Manele Bay, it's only about eight miles to Lahaina," Mike went on. "Though the race back to Honolulu doesn't launch until Monday, festivities start in earnest on Sat- urday, with the Lahaina Offshore Regatta. There tends to be very little wind off Lahaina in early September—eight knots might be better than average. A few years back, I started the routine of firing up a grill and barbecuing a meal in the course of the race. With such light wind, it's hard to take things too seriously. Sunday, events are brought on shore. All the sailors from Maui team up against all the sailors who've come over from Oahu—gener- ally, that would be visiting members of the Waikiki Yacht Club, the Hawaii Yacht Club, and the Kane'ohe Yacht Club. I can't speak to the level of softball that's played, but I can say that a good deal of beer is drunk . . . though not *too* much, as wake-up time on Monday is around five a.m. for the race, which begins at eight." If your visit to Lahaina doesn't coincide with the softball challenge, you might wish to take in Lahaina's Whaling Days and Whales Today museum, which chronicles the region's evolution from whaling ground to ecotourism playground. Ka'anapali Beach at Lahaina, voted one of the world's best beaches, may also merit a visit.

"The race itself poses one key question," Mike continued. "Do you sail north of Molokai or south of Molokai? If you sail north, you add an extra eight or ten miles to the trip, but you're treated to some exceptionally beautiful scenery, including a number of waterfalls. You also get steady wind. If you cut through the slot between Molokai and

Lanai, you save miles, but the odds are pretty good that you'll hit doldrums and spend an hour slatting around. It's a gamble—most people go north."

Racing is a big part of the Hawaiian sailing experience, but so is kicking back. "Fishing is a big part of any trip between the islands," Mike concluded. "Ahi, mahi mahi, and ono are all commonly caught. A dream cruise is to sail across the channel to Molokai or Lanai dragging a bait or lure, hook a mahi mahi, find a nice anchorage, watch the sunset, and grill that fish up and have it with a nice glass of wine."

Mike Rothwell is a fifth-generation Hawaiian, and grew up sailing on the waters of his native Oahu. He represented the United States in the 1976 Olympic Games in Montreal, competing in the Tornado class with David McFaul; their team won two silver medals. He is a past commodore of the Waikiki Yacht Club (his father and grandfather also served as commodores of the club), and also a member of the Hawaii Yacht Club and the Maui Boat and Yacht Club.

IF YOU GO

➤ **Getting There:** Service is provided to Honolulu, Oahu, by many major carriers, including American, Continental, Hawaiian, and Northwest Airlines.

➤ **Best Time to Visit:** Weather conditions are very consistent, with average daytime temps at sea level around 80°F. The summer months (May through October) tend to see less surf activity, and less rain. If you wish to partake in the festivities surrounding the Lahaina to Honolulu Return Regatta, visit Labor Day weekend.

➤ **Charter Operators:** The Honolulu Sailing Company (800-829-0114; www.honsail.com) has both bareboat and skippered charters available.

➤ **Moorings:** In Honolulu, visitor berths are available at several marinas and clubs, including Keehi Marine Center (808-845-6465; keehimarine.com) and Hawaii Yacht Club (808-949-4622, ext. 10; www.hawaiiyachtclub.org).

➤ **On-Shore Accommodations:** The Hawaii Visitors and Convention Bureau (800-464-2924; www.gohawaii.com) lists a full range of accommodations on all the islands.

21

DESTINATION

CHICAGO (LAKE MICHIGAN)

RECOMMENDED BY **Janet C. Baxter**

Janet Baxter's connection to Lake Michigan and the Chicago Yacht Club goes back as long as she can remember . . . perhaps even longer!

"My parents met at the harbor that's now across from my apartment," Janet began. "My dad raced little boats, my mom sailed big boats with her dad. Eventually, my dad ended up crewing on my mom's dad's boat. My grandfather—Jack Kinsey—was an extremely avid sailor, and once won the Mackinac Cup. I started sailing and racing at the Chicago Yacht Club at an early age. When I got a bit older, I crewed on my dad's boat. He was a man of great patience, and a wonderful teacher. He lost many races on account of his relatively unskilled family crew! Sailing has been a great common bond for our family, something to keep us together. And Lake Michigan has been a tremendous place to sail because it has all kinds of water—anything from flat calm in the a.m. to five-foot seas in the late afternoon."

It should come as no great surprise that Chicago, known in some circles as "The Windy City," has a strong sailing community and a long yachting history. If there's a center to Chicago's sailing scene, it would be the aforementioned Chicago Yacht Club. The club was formally established in 1875, though seeds for its creation were planted in 1869 when a Scottish immigrant named Joseph Ruff contracted with a boat builder named Michael Carson to construct an 18-foot catboat. Three similar sloops were soon built on the same model, and sailed frequently on Lake Michigan until the Chicago Fire in 1871. Today the club is a prominent player on the national yacht-racing scene, presenting the Verve Cup and NOOD for offshore racers, the Timme Angsten Regatta for collegiate sailors, and the North American Challenge Cup for disabled sailors. Sponsorship of this event has been fostered by the club's relationship with the Judd Goldman Adaptive Sailing Program, a

OPPOSITE
The Chicago Yacht Club Race to Mackinac is a highlight of the sailing season on Lake Michigan.

DESTINATION 22

public/private partnership with the Chicago Park District that provides sailing instruction for people with disabilities to help them achieve greater independence.

Oh yes, and they're involved in a little race that's affectionately called "The Mac."

Chicago Yacht Club's Race to Mackinac, billed as the world's longest annual freshwater race at 333 miles, dates back to 1898. Mackinac Island, resting just inside the perimeter of Lake Huron (just north of Lake Michigan), has been a popular vacation destination for the smart set since the 1870s, when 80 percent of the island was declared the nation's second national park (its ownership and management was later transferred to the state of Michigan). Many of the grandiose "cottages" built by the lumber and railroad barons of the day (among other captains of industry) remain today.

One of the distinctions that have marked The Mac over the years has been the severe conditions that can mar the progress of northward-bound sailors. Chicago Yacht Club records recount harrowing tales from four Mac races in particular. In 1911, eleven boats battled gusts that reached 80 miles an hour; one craft, the *Vanenna* (winner of the first Mac race), was eventually claimed by the storm, though the crew was rescued. In 1925, twenty-one boats started the race, though within twelve hours, six had been blown back to Chicago. In 1937, gusts up to 75 miles per hour made sailing nearly impossible; only eight boats out of forty-two starters finished the race. In 1970, 167 racers faced a northerly wind for sixteen hours, with gusts reaching 60 miles per hour; more than half of the participants ended up taking refuge from the gales in safe harbors.

"When I was thirteen or fourteen, I competed in my first Chicago-to-Mackinac race," Janet said. "I was a little scared about the possibility of bad weather, considering the race's history, but having sailed across the lake before, I was prepared. The weather was cooperative, and we finished intact. One aspect of The Mac that's particularly nice is that after the rigors of the race, you get to take your time and cruise home. There are some lovely little lakeside towns in the northern part of Lake Michigan—Harbor Springs, Leland, and Portage Lake are a few favorite stopovers. Late July [when The Mac takes place] is a wonderful time to be on the lake. The sun is out late, the air is warm, and despite those horror stories you hear, the weather is usually quite good."

The Chicago-to-Mackinac race has its share of endearing hallmarks. One is the "Island Goat Sailing Society." To be an "Island Goat," one must have competed in the The Mac at least twenty-five times, amassing a minimum of 8,325 northbound miles in the process. (The story goes that the name derives from a comment made by an onlooker at one event, that the sailors had been on the boat so long that they smelled like a bunch of goats!) The eldest "goat" to complete the race is a gentleman named Karl Stein, who participated in his ninety-sixth year. For Janet, there's a very personal Mac memory: "When my grandfather died, a trophy was donated to the Chicago Yacht Club in his name, and it became one of the trophies for the Chicago-to-Mackinac race. One year, our boat won our class in The Mac, and that brought us the Jack Kinsey trophy. Being presented my grandfather's trophy was especially touching for me and my family."

One need not compete in The Mac, however, to appreciate the joys of sailing Lake Michigan out of Chicago. "Just going out for an afternoon sail—or better yet, an evening sail—is fantastic," Janet added. "There's nothing quite like the skyline of Chicago from the water. You can sail from harbor to harbor, up and down the waterfront, and have a great time. As the sun goes down and the lights come up, it looks different every day. You don't notice the changes from shore—but from the water, it's spectacular."

Janet C. Baxter is the first woman president of US Sailing; during the day, she's a management consultant. Janet has served on the organization's board of directors in many roles. She has also served on the audit committee of the United States Olympic Committee. She races actively in Chicago, where she has participated in thirty Chicago-to-Mackinac races. She has raced a variety of offshore boats as well as Etchells, Lasers, and other dinghies.

◤ **IF YOU GO** ◢

➤ **Getting There:** Chicago is served by all major air carriers.

➤ **Best Time to Visit:** The Mac is run each year the last week in July. This is an excellent time to experience the Chicago sailing scene.

➤ **Charter Operators:** A number of companies offer charter sailing on Lake Michigan. Bareboat charters are available from Chicago Sailing (773-871-7245; www.chicagosailing. com).

➤ **Moorings:** The Chicago Harbors (312-742-8520; www.chicagoharbors.info) operates nine harbors on the lakefront. Moorings are often available for visitors.

➤ **On-Shore Accommodations:** The Chicago Convention and Tourism Bureau (877-244-2246; www.choosechicago.com) provides a good overview of accommodations options in the Windy City.

COSTA SMERALDA, SARDINIA

RECOMMENDED BY **Sean Healey**

The world's most finely engineered yachts crowding a picturesque Mediterranean harbor, framed by rocky hillsides. The docks overflowing with beautiful people, European jet-setters, nobility, and international celebrities. Fighter jets flying overhead.

It must be Sardinia!

"Sardinia—particularly Costa Smeralda—is not the kind of place where the average American would visit at the drop of a hat," Sean Healey began. "It's about the highest society I've ever experienced, and working on the Rolex circuit, I've been fortunate enough to visit some very nice places. Personalities like the late Princess Di vacation there. And when the races are on, royals from Europe's remaining monarchies might be there (hence the fighter jets). I've always been thankful that it's on the race circuit, or else I don't think I would've ever gotten to Sardinia; each time I'd come off the boat, I'd realize just how much the other crew members and I, in our dirty T-shirts and khaki shorts, didn't fit in . . . though after being there, I'd do anything to go back!"

Sardinia is the second-largest island in the Mediterranean Sea, located west of the Italian mainland, north of Tunisia, and just south of the French island of Corsica. The island is one of Italy's five autonomous regions, with its capital, Cagliari, in the far south. Through history, Sardinia has had a variety of courtesans and conquerors, including (but not limited to) the Phoenicians, Carthaginians, Romans, Byzantines, and, finally, the Italians. The island has been part of Italy since the early 1700s, and though Italian is widely spoken and many aspects of Italian culture have been adopted, Sardinian (an early Romance language dating back two thousand years) is still commonly heard.

Costa Smeralda (or "Emerald Coast") is on Sardinia's northeastern shore, and stretches roughly 30 miles, from the town of Palau to Olbia. The jagged, rugged shoreline

OPPOSITE
The Maxi Yacht
Rolex Cup
attracts the most
expensive boats
in the world to
Costa Smeralda.

23

DESTINATION

105

is punctuated by beautiful white sand beaches. The sailing focal point of Costa Smeralda is Porto Cervo, which is home to Yacht Club Costa Smeralda, sponsor of the Maxi Yacht Rolex Cup and the Rolex Sardinia Cup. Porto Cervo is a fairly recent construct of a development consortium led by Prince Karim Aga Khan IV—a fascinating man who is a billionaire sailor (he's currently president of the Yacht Club Costa Smeralda), a philanthropist, and the forty-ninth hereditary imam, a spiritual leader with lineage tracing directly to the prophet Muhammad. Prince Khan's vision of an elite retreat has been splendidly realized; Porto Cervo is among the most expensive resort towns in the world.

But no amount of money or glitterati can buy good sailing conditions. Fortunately, Costa Smeralda has been blessed in this respect as well.

"I'd have to say that Costa Smeralda is one of the nicest places in the world to sail—especially for deep-water draft boats," Sean opined. "The water is very deep in most places; it seems that if you step off the shoreline, you sink thirty feet. The race routes often weave right along the shoreline of channels and bays. Some of the channels are only a mile across. It's really something to see sixty boats, all sixty or eighty feet long, squeezing through; some boats are pushed right against the cliffs. Costa Smeralda is a windy place. When the mistral arrives [generally blowing from the northwest], it can blow up to forty or fifty miles per hour. From a racing perspective, going from the buoy course that's out in the open water around the La Maddalena archipelago to entering and exiting the bays keeps you on your toes. You have to be able to adjust quickly."

Of the Rolex events held around Costa Smeralda, the Maxi Yacht Rolex Cup—which dates back to 1980—is probably the most revered. Maxi racing, as the name implies, is for big boats. The current generation of Maxis take their inspiration from the America's Cup Class of boat that replaced the 12-meter boats that had been used through the 1987 cup race. Where 80-foot boats were once at the high end of the Maxi class, most boats racing at Sardinia now approach or eclipse 100 feet. Events are held for five divisions: the Racing Division (for the highest-performance racing yachts, minimum of 80 feet in length); the Cruising Division (high-performance boats with luxurious cabins, minimum 80 feet in length); the W Division (racers have their own handicap system based on the IMS Velocity Prediction Program); the Spirit of Tradition (built to look old fashioned, but employing modern keel configurations); and the Mini Max (like the Racing Division craft, but between 60 and 79 feet in length). "It's one thing to compete against some of the world's greatest sailors at an event like the Maxi," Sean said. "But the boats are incredible."

"When the Maxi Yacht Rolex Cup is occurring, all the boats are moored in front of the Yacht Club Costa Smeralda, all with their sterns pointed out. You have a half-mile-long row of some of the finest sailboats in the world. When the boats are coming in from the last race of the day, the thing to do for Porto Cervo's visitors is to come down to the pier and check out the boats. In the States, sailing isn't much of a spectator sport, so we're not used to having much interest. But there on the pier at Porto Cervo are some of the most beautiful people in the world, dressed to the nines, watching to see which boats return first and then checking out the craft. It's about as glamorous as sailing can get."

Sean Healey is a professional sailor and marine electronics specialist based in Portsmouth, Rhode Island. He currently works with E2 Marine Electronics (www.e2marine.com), which provides instrumentation installation and support for customers in General Handicap fleets, One-Design fleets, Grand Prix IMS, Volvo Ocean Races, and America's Cup campaigns.

▶ IF YOU GO

➤ **Getting There:** Costa Smeralda is served by the airport at Olbia. Most international travelers will fly to Milan, and then on to Olbia. Service to Olbia is offered by several local carriers, including Air Dolomiti (+39 45 288 6140; www.airdolomiti.it).

➤ **Best Time to Visit:** Sardinia has a Mediterranean climate, with the warmest, driest weather in the summer. Racing reaches its peak in September.

➤ **Charter Operators:** Bareboat charters on Costa Smeralda are available through Yacht-Booker Yacht Charter (+49 89 420 959 871 0; www.yachtbooker.com).

➤ **Moorings:** You'll pay a premium for a berth around Porto Cervo. One place to try is Marina Porto Cervo (+39 789 91100).

➤ **On-Shore Accommodations:** Sardegna.com (www.sardegna.com) is a good jumping-off point for finding on-shore lodgings.

BOOTHBAY HARBOR

RECOMMENDED BY **Timothy S. Hodgdon**

The town of Boothbay Harbor, situated about 40 miles east of Portland at the beginning of mid-coast Maine, has capitalized on its exquisite scenery and quaint Yankee ambiance better than many similar towns along the coast. It's a regular stop for tour bus operators after leaving L. L. Bean in Freeport; it fills its excursion boats and hotel rooms day in and day out from July through September. It supports many of the purveyors of saltwater taffy, T-shirts, and discounted shoes that a tourist town inevitably attracts.

And despite the crowds and the slightest tinge of commercial tackiness, its namesake harbor, the scores of islands, and the hundreds of miles of coves and inlets that surround it are still a joy to sail.

"I grew up on Linekin Bay, the bay east of Boothbay Harbor," Tim Hodgdon began. "I had lobster traps as a boy, sailed little sailboats, and zipped around in Boston Whalers and lobster skiffs. I was always around the water. My family's shipyard was on the Damariscotta River, the next big inlet up the coast, just a stone's throw from Linekin Bay. When I was a little older, I left for a time and did some different things, including working on an offshore lobster boat 120 miles off Cape Cod on the edge of the continental shelf. But I knew I'd always come back to Boothbay."

The greater Boothbay region can be loosely defined as the area between the Sheepscot River's entrance to the Atlantic to the west, and Monhegan Island to the east. As much as any section of the Maine coast, Boothbay is tremendously indented with bays and coves, offering shelter from heavy winds and rough seas—and almost unlimited exploring opportunities. "I spent my childhood gunkholing around Linekin Bay, the Damariscotta River, and the Sheepscot River. You can explore forever; there are so many spots to poke into."

OPPOSITE
An abundance of small islands is one of the charms of sailing around Boothbay Harbor.

DESTINATION 24

The inner sanctum of Boothbay Harbor is as pretty a Maine harbor as you could hope for. On your right is Brown Brothers Wharf, a marina/restaurant/hotel marked by a statue of a giant yellow-coated fisherman; it was featured in the 1956 musical *Carousel*. On the left is the downtown area, anchored by Fisherman's Wharf restaurant/hotel and the town's public docks. Straight ahead are several commercial fishing docks flanking Our Lady Queen of Peace Catholic Church, a sanctuary so stunningly white that it shines like an advertisement for Weatherbeater paint, eternal salvation, or both. Fishing still matters in the community, and moorings in the harbor are split between lobster boats and sloops.

When you move outside of the harbor proper, beyond the reach of the aforementioned tour buses, the Boothbay area takes on a more relaxed, indolent air. Linekin Bay, Ocean Point, Five Islands, Southport—these are the spots where summer is as much a verb as a season. Long-term vacationers from Connecticut, Massachusetts, New York, and beyond occupy the summer homes here as they have for generations, dutifully sending their children to sailing camp at the Boothbay Harbor or Southport Yacht Club. Others sail and summer on one of the many islands that dot the waters outside the harbor—Squirrel (named for its shape as seen from above), Negro (as it was once a stop on the Underground Railroad for escaped slaves bound for Canada), Damariscove, or better-known Monhegan. One venue that captures the feeling of this bygone era of summer vacations is the Linekin Bay Resort. For sixty years, the resort has catered to vacationers, providing lodge and cabin rooms, communal meals, and relaxed sailing instruction. Guests can avail themselves of a dinghy from the largest resort sailing fleet on the East Coast, swim in a heated saltwater pool, or simply watch the gulls wheel against the blue sky.

When asked about a favorite day sail, Tim was hard pressed. "I don't know that there's one perfect day out there," he said. "I love going up through the Townsend Gut—where the Sheepscot River flows toward Boothbay Harbor—and then on across the Sheepscot River to Five Islands, and up the Sasanoa River to Bath. Going a little further south, it's great fun to go ashore on Seguin Island, near the mouth of the Kennebec. The lighthouse there is one of the oldest in the country, commissioned in 1795. These spots are more inland; if I'm in more of an ocean mood and the weather cooperates, I might head out to Damariscove or Outer Heron Island. They're about three or four miles out, and both have protected coves with nice anchorages, although Damariscove is a safer anchorage in some conditions. If time allowed, I would head east to Muscongus Bay, an area with a vast number of unique spots to explore."

A sailing event that's special to Tim is the Shipyard Cup, which is hosted by Hodgdon Yachts and various other sponsors. This regatta is open to yachts over 70 feet and is held the first weekend after Labor Day, with races conducted at various sites in the Boothbay region. "Our intention all along has been to keep this a low-key, good-fun sailboat racing weekend," Tim explained. "On the Friday before the racing starts, there's a clambake in front of the shipyard in East Boothbay for participants; Shipyard Brewing Company provides the beer. Saturday there's racing, then a rendezvous in Boothbay Harbor for cocktails and dinner. Sunday there's another race, then an awards ceremony to wrap up the event. Win or lose, everyone enjoys the weekend on the spectacular coast of Maine."

Timothy S. Hodgdon is the president and CEO of Hodgdon Yachts, a fifth-generation, 190-year-old family business based in East Boothbay, Maine. Hodgdon Shipbuilding began in 1816; currently the company has hulls #406 and #407 under construction. Notable yachts built by Hodgdon Yachts in recent years include the 80-foot commuter-style M/Y *Liberty*, the 124-foot sloop *Antonisa*, and the 155-foot ketch *Scheherazade*. Hodgdon Yachts has received the Governor's Award for Business Excellence by then-governor Angus King. In addition to his responsibilities at Hodgdon Yachts, Tim is chairman of the board of Maine Marine Manufacturing LLC (MMM), a marketing and contracting entity formed as a result of Hodgdon Yachts Inc.'s entrance into DOD and other commercial contracting ventures. He is also a founding member and manager of the Shipyard Cup.

IF YOU GO

➤ **Getting There:** The greater Boothbay region is 40 miles north of Portland, which is served by many major carriers, including Continental, Delta, and United Airlines.
➤ **Best Time to Visit:** Prime time is July and August, though the crowds lessen (and some years the weather improves) in September.
➤ **Charter Operators:** Points East Sailing (207-633-4436; www.pointseastsailing.com) has limited bareboat charters available.
➤ **Moorings:** Many options are available in and around Boothbay Harbor. You may wish to begin with a call to Boothbay Harbor's harbor master, Earl Brown, at 207-633-5281.
➤ **On-Shore Accommodations:** The Maine Office of Tourism (888-624-6345; www.visitmaine.com) has a comprehensive list of options.

PENOBSCOT BAY

RECOMMENDED BY **John Worth**

✳

For more than thirty years, John Worth has seen Penobscot Bay from the decks of tugboats, tall ships, and one-of-a-kind Arctic schooners. He hasn't tired of the view yet.

"I've been sailing Penobscot Bay since 1973," John said, "and I have to say that I love this place. I'm out here all the time; I commute to work by boat, work on a boat, and sail for pleasure. Penobscot Bay gives you tremendous sailing variety. Thanks to its glacial formation, the bay is very long and wide. There can be a significant ocean swell on the seaward side, but it's like a lake near the mainland around Castine and Searsport. If you're inclined, you can also experience the river phenomenon by going up the Penobscot River. You've got brown water going to fresh water to blue/green water to seawater. The water is so deep you can bring a boat—even a large boat like a windjammer—very close to shore."

Penobscot Bay is in the geographic center of the Maine coast, and in some ways likewise captures the gestalt of the Pine Tree State. Forty miles long and fifteen miles wide, dotted by over two hundred islands, the Bay is a mélange of hard-working fishing villages, tourist towns, summer retreats, and secluded harbors—in short, a cruiser's dream come true. "I captained vessels and ran a windjammer business from 1973 to 1984," John continued, "and I could always find new places to explore. You can start from Belfast Bay in the northwestern section of the bay and find a protected cove every few miles. You don't have to think too much about where you're going to stop because there are so many sheltered, beautiful places to anchor. All day long, you can be saying to yourself, 'I can make place A or place B, depending on the wind.' You know you're not going to get stuck. This is very desirable. Plus, the wind in the summer cruising season is moderate and predictable; you can start out in the late morning, puttering, and pretty much count on a

OPPOSITE
At the geographic center of coastal Maine, Penobscot Bay captures the region's gestalt.

DESTINATION 25

three p.m. wind to bring you back in. That's not to say that the sailing is always easy. There are a lot of rocks, and lots of current thanks to considerable tides. Everything is well buoyed, however, and the prudent mariner should have no problem finding his or her way around. There are many uninhabited areas, and they're staying pristine. Cruisers are working with landowners through an organization called the Maine Island Trails Association to promote conservation while giving sailors access. Maine has a reputation for understanding and protecting its resources. The Association is a good example of this enlightened stewardship."

The remarkable scenery of the region—evergreen and hardwood forests, granite hills and sparkling blue waters—is best summed up by the poet Edna St. Vincent Millay:

> All I could see from where I stood
> was three long mountains and a wood
> I turned and looked the other way
> and saw three islands and a bay.

Incidentally, Millay called the Camden/Rockland region home.

While the villages on the mainland along Penobscot Bay—from charming Rockport and Camden in the southwest to the working harbors of Belfast and Castine to the north—certainly add to the region's appeal, it is the many islands that dot the bay that perhaps provide its greatest allure. Some of the islands are served by frequent ferry runs, and hence are a bit more connected to mainland life; others, like Isle au Haut, can only be reached by a mailboat out of Stonington, or by private craft. The Fox Islands, North Haven and Vinalhaven, seem to capture two of the distinct faces of the region. North Haven, like Southwest Harbor to the north, is an affluent summer community populated for the most part by seasonal out-of-staters. (Pulpit Harbor on the northwestern part of the island is a favorite anchoring place for cruisers.) Across the Fox Island Thoroughfare is Vinalhaven, which was once a significant producer of granite, shipped as far south as New Orleans. (Many of the island and mainland communities were active in the granite industry.) Today it remains a working island; picturesque Carvers Harbor is home to one of Maine's most prolific lobster industries.

"My favorite of the islands is Deer Isle," John commented. "Fishing is still its bread and butter, but the island has welcomed vacationers as well. It seems like the two sometimes competing interests are working together now. Though it's worlds away in some ways, Deer Isle is only a twenty-six-mile cruise from Camden. The proximity of everything in Penobscot Bay is one of its most attractive features."

When many think of the Maine Coast, the image of tall ships billows before their eyes. The fourteen ships hailing from the ports of Rockland, Rockport, and Camden that make up the Maine Windjammer Association call Penobscot Bay home. These ships range from 46 to 132 feet, and include craft that first set sail in 1871. Some were used for fishing and carrying cargo, while others were built for the windjammer trade. All have been lovingly and traditionally maintained. If you don't have time or inclination to sail Penobscot Bay on your own, the windjammer fleet provides an excellent alternative. "It's an all-encompassing experience," John said. "Guests are asked to leave their radios and cell phones on shore and immerse themselves in life on the boat. You smell the wood stove, help set the sails, soak in the whole ambiance. Some people gravitate toward helping in the galley, some toward helping sail the vessel, others toward lying in the sun. You can make of it what you want, and that's the beauty of it."

Considering Maine's long seafaring history (the first English ship built in America, the *Virginia*, was launched here in 1607), it's not surprising that the state's coast is home to a first-rate nautical institution—the Maine Maritime Academy. Established in 1941, the Academy operates out of Castine, and annually graduates upward of two hundred students a year with degrees ranging from marine engineering to small-craft design. Sailing is offered as part of the curriculum through several P.E. classes, though the Academy's best-known ambassador to sailing has been the *Bowdoin*, a schooner built in 1921 at East Boothbay's Hodgdon Brothers Shipyard to ply Arctic waters. Since that time, she's made twenty-eight trips north of the Arctic Circle. The *Bowdoin* has been honored as a floating national historic landmark and as the official sailing craft of the great state of Maine. Each summer, she's used in a variety of educational settings. In the summer, John Worth is at her helm.

John Worth began his marine career in the windjammer vacation business in Camden, Maine, in 1973, serving as captain of the Schooner *Mistress* and then the *Mercantile*. He rebuilt a 1911 sardine carrier, the *Sylvina W. Beal*, and operated her out of Belfast, Maine, for four years. A chance trip to Eastport driving the tug *Brian F.* led to a career change. In 1989, John bought a tugboat company and launched Maineport Towboats. For fourteen years, he operated this company, docking and sailing ships in Bucksport and Searsport, Bath, Portland, and Portsmouth, New Hampshire. During off hours, he worked as relief captain for the schooners *Timberwind* and *Stephen Taber*; he has a 1,600-ton master steam and motor, with a towing endorsement and a 100-ton auxiliary sail, and a U.S.C.G. license. John joined the Maine Maritime Academy in 2003 as a small-craft master and adjunct instructor. He teaches tug and barge operations and work-boat operations. He is captain of the schooner *Bowdoin* and is involved in the Academy's traditional sail programs. On the *Bowdoin*, he captains the annual small-vessel operations cruise to Nova Scotia, oversees the schooner crew team, and plans and carries out summer and fall training and development trips. Captain Worth is married, with two children. His wife is a Maine District Court judge. His son, a graduate of the U.S. Military Academy at West Point, is a lieutenant in the U.S. Army. His daughter, a member of the class of 2008, University of Pennsylvania, worked as a cook aboard the schooner *Bowdoin* in the summer of 2006.

IF YOU GO

➤ **Getting There:** The towns of Rockland and Camden are approximately 100 miles north of Portland, which is served by many major carriers, including Continental, Delta, and United Airlines. Belfast is a bit closer to Bangor, which is served by American, Continental, and Delta.

➤ **Best Time to Visit:** July and August are major tourist times and offer fairly consistent weather. September can be an excellent time to be on the water here.

➤ **Charter Operators:** Johanson Boatworks (877-4JOHANS; www.jboatworks.com) in Rockland has many bareboat charter boats available. Gafia Sailing Charters (207-323-4800; www.gafia.com) offers skippered charters from Belfast.

➤ **Moorings:** Many options are available on Penobscot Bay. In Camden, Wayfarer Marine (www.wayfarermarine.com) offers moorings. In Belfast, contact the harbor master, Katherine Messier, at 207-388-1142 for mooring information.

➤ **On-Shore Accommodations:** Rockland, Camden, Belfast, and Castine all cater to visitors. The Maine Office of Tourism (888-624-6345; www.visitmaine.com) has a comprehensive list of lodgings options.

SOUTHWEST HARBOR

RECOMMENDED BY **Jennifer French**

Southwest Harbor is situated in the region that's come to be called "Downeast" Maine. As the editors of *DownEast* magazine explain, the term used to refer to the entire state of Maine—a place that sailing ships leaving Boston reached by sailing downwind to the east (residents were called *Downeasters*). In more recent times, however, the term has come to reference the coast east of Ellsworth, a rugged and relatively remote section of the Pine Tree State.

"I first heard about Southwest Harbor from a cruising friend who'd just returned from Downeast Maine," Jennifer French recalled. "He said, 'This is where you need to be.' I hadn't gotten the racing bug yet, and was doing a lot of cruising at that time. When my next vacation came, I headed up there. It was challenging sailing at times—you really have to know your navigation tools, because when the fog comes in, your visibility goes down to zero. But the region's beauty and unique personality made the challenges worthwhile."

Like so much of the Maine coast, the Downeast region is carved with countless coves, bays, harbors, and estuaries; while there are less than 250 road miles along Route 1 from Kittery to Eastport, the coastline is over 3,000 miles were you to traverse every inch by water—not to mention myriad small islands. With so many places to tuck into, it's no wonder that Maine is a cruiser's haven. There's a great deal to see; but one must also be prepared to see a great deal of the same thing. "If a fog bank rolls in, you might find yourself in a harbor for a few days," Jen explained. "If that happens, you'll learn the intricacies of the harbor and the town. If you're sailing in the vicinity of Southwest Harbor, you'll do well not to schedule yourself too tightly. You need to leave a block of time to sit and wait if the fog comes in. If I'm going up there, I like to give myself two weeks to account for the possibility of uncertain weather. Another thing you need to be conscious of when you're sailing in Downeast Maine are the tides, which can be as much as seventeen feet. The tides and weather, sunrise and sunset dictate your schedule more than what your watch says."

Most cruisers departing from Southwest Harbor will wend their way slowly east, perhaps beginning with a brief detour to Bass Harbor on the south end of Mt. Desert Island. Bass Harbor is the archetypal lobster fishing village, with white lobster boats and multi-hued buoys bobbing against a background of spruce and clapboard houses. Many don't realize that Friendship Sloops got their start in the late 1800s as the craft of choice for lobstermen (they were sometimes called lobster sloops). It wasn't until after World War II that engine-powered lobster boats began to replace sail- and oar-powered craft. "If we stop in Bass Harbor," Jen said, "we almost always stop at Thurston's Lobster Pound. It's pretty barebones, with little plastic forks, and steamed lobsters served whole, with a little cup of butter to dip the meat in. If you like lobster, it's your kind of place, and they serve good beer to wash it all down."

Heading back east toward Acadia, Somes Sound is worth a stop; it's the only fjord on the eastern seaboard. "It's like you're in Norway or Finland—you go up this river with steep cliffs that opens up to this sound," Jen added. "There is lots of birdlife, including bald eagles. If you like to hike or bike, a stop-off at Acadia is a must." Acadia is the first national park that was established east of the Mississippi, its 47,000 acres set aside in 1919 by President Woodrow Wilson when the park was called Lafayette (the name changed in 1929). Hiking to the top of Cadillac Mountain (at 1,532 feet, the tallest point along the eastern seaboard) to take in the sunrise is a treasured experience for visitors; from this vista point in the far-eastern reaches of the U.S., you'll be among the first of your countrymen to greet the day!

After a day or two in Acadia, some cruisers will spend an afternoon or evening in Bar Harbor. While it has largely evolved into a tourist destination, Bar Harbor has a rich past. At one time, it rivaled Newport as a summering place for society people; indeed, many of the families who maintained homes in Newport kept "cottages" on Mt. Desert Island as well. Various Vanderbilts and other luminaries of the gilded age were drawn to Bar Harbor by the paintings of a group of artists from the Hudson River School, sometimes called "the rusticators"—including Frederic Church, Thomas Cole, and William Hart—who captured the region's beauty in their work. "There aren't many towns once you push east from Bar Harbor," Jen said. "We like to stop in for an evening of civilized fun—including a stop at the Thirsty Whale, a favorite pub—before continuing on."

One may very well find little use for towns when hideaways like Roque Island await. "Roque Island is one of my favorite places," Jen continued. "Most cruisers to the region know it. It's a little horseshoe-shaped island [actually a series of islands], with a number of little coves you can tuck into. One remarkable feature is the long, white sandy beach on the main island. You don't see many white beaches in Maine—in fact, I can't think of any I've encountered. It's reminiscent of the Caribbean, except with pine trees and cold water."

Whether at the beginning of your trip or at its conclusion, you should consider a stop at one or two of Southwest Harbor's eminent yacht builders; one nautical writer has called the town the home of the world's best boat builders. Residents include Morris Yachts, Ralph Stanley Boat Builders, John M. Williams Boat Yard, Ellis Boat Builders, Malcolm L. Pettegrow, Inc., Lee S. Wilbur & Co., and Jarvis Newman Boats. Best known among Southwest Harbor's boat builders is the Hinckley Company, which dates back to 1928, making it one of the country's oldest yacht builders. Hinckley made a name for itself constructing high-quality production boats, including the Bermuda 40, the Sou'wester 30, and the Hinckley 41.

Downeasters have a reputation for being a little aloof and suspicious of outsiders; perhaps this attitude was fostered a century ago when wealthy city folk came in and bought up all the shorefront land and posted "No Trespassing" signs. But Jen has found that while Mainers may size you up, they're more than willing to give you the benefit of the doubt. "If you're willing to help Mainers out, they're willing to help you," she explained. "One day, we were trying to find a hurricane hole as a big front was coming through. We came into a little cove where there was a bunch of lobstermen around. There were no moorings for visitors, but we offered to do some work for them in exchange for use of one of their moorings. Things worked out fine."

Jennifer French acquired her C6–7 incomplete spinal-cord injury as a result of a snowboarding accident in 1998. Prior to her injury, she was recreationally active with such sports as canoeing, snowboarding/skiing, sailing, fly fishing, scuba diving/snorkeling, and biking. Since her injury, Jennifer still participates in all those activities. She is an active user of FES systems. In November 1999, she received the Implantable Standing and

Transfer System provided by the Cleveland FES Center—the first woman to receive such a system. Now residing in St. Petersburg, Florida, Jennifer is actively involved with the community sailing program and is a member of the U.S. Disabled Sailing Team. Over the course of her career, Jennifer has helped launch successful divisions in such organizations as Bombardier Capital and PC Connection, Inc. With an M.B.A., she works with profit and nonprofit organizations and freelances her talents through TJF Consulting, Inc. As a user of neurotechnology who has reaped its benefits, she is the cofounder of a nonprofit organization, Neurotech Network. Most recently, Jennifer's story was featured in the documentary film *To Have Courage*.

IF YOU GO

➤ **Getting There:** Southwest Harbor is approximately 140 miles north of Portland, which is served by many major carriers, including Continental, Delta, and United Airlines. It's about 50 miles from Bangor, which is served by American, Continental, and Delta.

➤ **Best Time to Visit:** July and August are major tourist times and offer fairly consistent weather. September can be an excellent time to be on the water here, though fog is an ever-present possibility.

➤ **Charter Operators:** Hinckley Yacht Charters (800-492-7245; www.hinckleycharters. com) has many boats available for Downeast cruising.

➤ **Moorings:** Most towns along this section of "Downeast Maine" offer moorings of one sort or another. In Southwest Harbor, you might begin with the harbor master, Gene Thurston, at 207-244-7913.

➤ **On-Shore Accommodations:** Southwest Harbor and nearby Bar Harbor offer many lodgings options. The Maine Office of Tourism (888-624-6345; www.visitmaine.com) has a comprehensive list.

DESTINATION

26

ANNAPOLIS

RECOMMENDED BY **William Chambers**

The sheltered waters of the northern Chesapeake Bay were explored by Captain John Smith (of Pocahontas fame) in the autumn of 1608 in a 30-foot shallop, a sailing/rowing boat of the day. Smith toured more than 1,500 miles of the bay with a crew of up to fifteen men in his shallop, and would later conclude that "no place is more convenient for pleasure, profit, and man's sustenance" than the Chesapeake Bay.

Some 370 years later, William Chambers arrived at much the same conclusion.

"After college, I took a position at Johns Hopkins," Bill recounted. "I knew nothing about sailing, but figured that since I was going to be so close to the Chesapeake Bay, I'd be foolish not to learn about it. I picked up a seventy-five-cent book with a title like *How to Sail* and began to figure it out. I started with a sixteen-foot Oslo, then moved up to a twenty-four-foot Rainbow. Pretty soon a coworker asked me to crew, and I got into racing. Annapolis is a wonderful place to race and crew, as there's something going on almost every weekend in one class or another within striking distance of Annapolis. With something like four thousand places to drop anchor, cruising on the bay is magnificent too."

Few would dispute that Annapolis is the hub of the mid-Atlantic sailing community (though citizens of Newport might have a thing or two to say about Annapolis's moniker, "America's Sailing Capital"). Prominent events like the Star Class World Championship, the Rolex International Women's Keelboat Championship, and the Annapolis Newport Race are organized by the Annapolis Yacht Club, which has been extremely active in promoting the furtherance of sailboat racing. The city is also home to one of America's most prominent sailing schools, the Annapolis Sailing School. Oh yes, and there's a little college here that's been known to produce a few sailors.

And then there's the Chesapeake itself. The watershed, which is the largest estuary in the United States, is long and narrow—200 miles long and ranging from just over 3 to 35 miles wide. The watershed includes parts of Delaware, Maryland, New York, Pennsylvania, Virginia, and West Virginia, and all of the District of Columbia. All but the southern portions of the bay are buffered from the Atlantic by the eastern shores of Maryland and Virginia. Nearly one-third of the population of the United States resides within a four-hour drive of some portion of the Chesapeake. Yet with 11,684 miles of shoreline, it's very possible to find a peaceful anchorage. "The water is quite shallow through most of the bay," Bill continued. "And the water never gets too rough. Sailing out of Annapolis, even a novice would be hard-pressed to find threatening water."

As alluded to above, the presence of the United States Naval Academy in Annapolis has certainly added to Annapolis's élan as a sailing center. There's an interesting story behind the birth of the Academy: Before its founding in 1845, there was no formal naval training program. Instead, teenage apprentices were taken out on "school ships" where hopefully they'd be inspired to embark on a naval career. In 1842, one such ship sailing from Brooklyn, the *American Brig Somers*, experienced a breakdown in discipline that eventually led to an attempted mutiny. The three perpetrators were hung from the ship's yardarm, and the whole incident caused officials to question the current mode of "on-board" education. This led Secretary of the Navy George Bancroft, who had a lifelong interest in furthering secondary education, to establish the Naval School in Annapolis, removed from "the temptations and distractions that necessarily connect with a large and populous city." By 1850 the Naval School became the United States Naval Academy, with a four-year curriculum that included on-ship training in the summers. Sailing is still part of the curriculum at Annapolis; all incoming midshipmen learn to command a small sailboat during their first three months, and a summer program—the Command Seamanship Navigation Training Squadron (conducted with the Naval Academy Sailing Squadron)—is attended by nearly nine hundred midshipmen, who sail along the East Coast in Navy 44 sloops.

While Annapolis is the site for some high-profile races, a favorite nautical amusement for many Annapolites—including Bill Chambers—is the Wednesday night races sponsored by the Annapolis Yacht Club. The races date back to the 1950s, and often include 150 boats participating in six classes. "The Wednesday night races are quite a spectacle," Bill said. "You'll have a whole assortment of boats out there, from sixty-foot cruising

OPPOSITE
Annapolis has
an active regatta
schedule for
racers and an
abundance of
calm waters for
cruisers.

DESTINATION

27

123

vessels to J/22s. The races start in Severin River, then the course brings racers by Spa Creek, and they end right in front of the Yacht Club. Spectators take in the race from all along the waterfront—by the Naval Academy seawall, on Spa Creek Bridge, from City Dock, or from the restaurants along the harbor. If you're a visitor cruising through the Greater Annapolis area, the Wednesday night races are something to be experienced."

William Chambers is a native of West Virginia, and worked as a researcher at Johns Hopkins University until retiring in 2000. He has been a competitive racer for many years, participating in the Annapolis to Cape May, Annapolis to Newport, and Marblehead to Bermuda races—not to mention a few Wednesday night events at the Annapolis Yacht Club. Bill has also sailed in New England, the Maritimes, Florida, and the U.S. Virgin Islands. He became active in administration of the Annapolis Yacht Club in 2000, holding various posts, including vice commodore and commodore.

▶ IF YOU GO

➤ **Getting There:** Annapolis is almost equidistant from Dulles International Airport and Baltimore Washington International Airport, both served by most major carriers.

➤ **Best Time to Visit:** Annapolis weather is conducive to sailing from mid-spring through October; it can be a bit warm and humid in midsummer.

➤ **Charter Operators:** Several outfits charter sailboats out of Annapolis, including Annapolis Sailing School (800-638-9192; www.annapolissailing.com), Chesapeake Boating Club at J-Port (410-280-2038; www.chesapeakeboatingclub.com), and SunSail (888-350-3568; www.sunsail.com).

➤ **Moorings:** Moorings and assorted nautical services are plentiful around greater Annapolis. A few options include Annapolis City Marina (410-268.0660; www.marinas.com/annapoliscitymarina), Annapolis Landing Marina (410-263-0090; www.annapolismarina.com/index.html), and Hinckley Yacht Services (410-226-5113; www.hinckleyyachts.com).

➤ **On-Shore Accommodations:** Annapolis is a popular tourist spot, and the city's many lodgings options are outlined at the Annapolis and Anne Arundel County Conference and Visitors Bureau (888-302-2852; www.visitannapolis.org).

BUZZARDS BAY

RECOMMENDED BY **Peter Mello**

Peter Mello grew up a stone's throw from one of New England's great sailing meccas. But it took some special circumstances to get him out on the water.

"I grew up in Fairhaven, Massachusetts, which is right on Buzzards Bay," Peter began. "Though my dad did some sailing, I was much more interested in baseball and football. When I was thirteen, my parents asked me out of the blue if I wanted to go to Tabor Academy—a college prep school, just up the coast in Marion. I thought for a while, and decided I'd try it. Sports are a mandatory activity at Tabor, and I needed to choose one. I put in for sailing on the school's tall ship, *Tabor Boy*. While the other guys were getting cleats and jockstraps, we got rigging knives and navy surplus jackets. When I went out to the boat that first day with the other recruits, I was welcomed aboard by what looked like a group of men (actually, they were just seniors). After a brief tour of the boat—a 128-foot-tall sail schooner—I was handed some sandpaper to sand the bulwarks. When we rookies got good at that, we were handed a paint brush, and then a varnishing brush. We learned by doing. In my freshman year, I knew nothing; by senior year, I was a fairly accomplished sailor. Those early days on Buzzards Bay helped shape what would become my vocation—leading the largest sail training association in the world."

Buzzards Bay is tucked between the western base of Cape Cod to the north, the Elizabeth Islands to the east, and the southeastern coast of Massachusetts to the west. The Bay is just northeast of the border with Rhode Island. It's approximately 28 miles long and averages 8 miles in width, with more than 350 miles of coastline. Eleven municipalities grace the bay, including the notable nautical towns of Marion, New Bedford, Padanaram, and Mattapoisett. It's believed that the region took its name from a colonist's mistaken identification of an osprey. Relatively shallow and shielded from the open

DESTINATION

28

Atlantic by the Elizabeths, Buzzards Bay has long been popular with sailors. "There's a pretty consistent southwest wind on Buzzards Bay," Peter continued. "If you sail from the mainland, this wind makes it pretty easy to get home at the end of the day."

With upward of ten thousand boats registered in its waters, Buzzards Bay supports a healthy competitive sailing program. Two events particularly stand out—the Buzzards Bay Regatta and the Marion to Bermuda Race. The Buzzards Bay Regatta originated in 1972 in an effort to rally a critical racing mass. At the time, individual clubs were having a difficult time getting enough entrants to make for an interesting race. So Bill Saltonstall (of the Beverly Yacht Club) and Bob Saltmarsh (of the New Bedford Yacht Club) helped unite all the bay's clubs for one big race. The first event was a grand success, and the concept has had staying power; today, 420 boats competing in fifteen classes make this regatta, held the first weekend in August, the largest multiclass event of its kind in the United States. The Marion to Bermuda Race launches from Buzzards Bay in odd-numbered years, and is geared toward cruising yachts. It's a joint effort of the Beverly Yacht Club, the Blue Water Sailing Club, and the Royal Hamilton Amateur Dinghy Club.

But it's not all racing around Buzzards Bay. For a pleasurable day cruise, Peter—like many other Buzzards Bay regulars—enjoys a sail out to the Elizabeth Islands. The Elizabeths are a chain of eight small islands: Naushon, Weepeckts, Pasque, Nashawena, Penikese, Cuttyhunk, Nonamesset, and Uncatena. All the islands, with the exception of Cuttyhunk and Penikese, are owned by the Forbes family (no relation to Malcolm or Steve). "I like to approach the islands from the southwest," Peter said. "I'd come in at Cuttyhunk, and sail right along the shorelines of Nashawena, then Naushon. You'll often see deer; you won't see many people aside from other boaters. You don't find many places in southern New England that are as unpopulated as those southern Elizabeth Islands— basically, it's twenty miles of uninhabited coastline." Of the Elizabeths, Cuttyhunk is the most accessible, with much of the land open to the public. "Cuttyhunk is a peaceful throwback to a quieter time," Peter added. "It's pretty difficult to get there if you don't go by boat."

As many may recall from their high-school reading of *Moby Dick*, New Bedford was once the whaling capital of the world. New Bedford began its rise to prominence as a whaling port in the mid-1700s as whalers looked to the open seas for their primary prey, sperm whales, which were prized for their clean-burning oil and their spermaceti (a substance found in the whale's head), which was used in the production of

OPPOSITE
With more than 10,000 sailboats registered in the area, Buzzards Bay can support a healthy racing schedule.

DESTINATION

28

127

fine candles. The Revolutionary War and the War of 1812 put a damper on the whaling industry, but once hostilities with England were settled, New Bedford entered its golden years, building its whaling fleet to thirty-six ships by 1820, seventy-five by 1841, and 329 by 1857. (Many of the ships were built in neighboring Mattapoisett.) At that time, more than ten thousand men were employed in New Bedford's whaling industry. A combination of factors—including the discovery of petroleum in Pennsylvania, losses suffered in the Civil War, the invention of the electric light, and the industry's inability to embrace new technology—all contributed to whaling's decline in New Bedford and other New England ports. The high and low points of the region's rich whaling history are nicely chronicled at the New Bedford Whaling Museum. "The museum is really amazing," Peter said enthusiastically. "Among other exhibits, there's a half-scale tall ship inside the building." Should you happen by New Bedford in January, you may have a chance to take part in the annual *Moby Dick* Marathon, where Melville's entire opus is read by 150 participants over the course of twenty-five hours.

Peter Mello started his career with tall ships in 1973 at the age of thirteen, as a freshman at Tabor Academy. In his senior year, he was elected by his peers as executive officer of the 128-foot square topsail schooner *Tabor Boy*. While a student at Connecticut College, he sat for his master's license and served as the Cuttyhunk ferry-boat captain during summer breaks, and restored antique boats at Classic Boat Works in Mystic, Connecticut, during the school year. Upon graduating, Peter embarked on a 20-year career in marine insurance and reinsurance, working in New York, Boston, San Francisco, St. Louis, and London. In his last position in this field, he served as president, chief operating officer, and partner of an international risk management and insurance services organization. In January 2001, Peter joined the American Sail Training Association as executive director and board member. He is the U.S. representative on the International Council of Sail Training International (a U.K. charity that promotes sail training globally), where he also chairs the International Trainee Exchange Program. He is an overseer of the Sea Education Association (SEA) in Woods Hole, Massachusetts, and serves on the Headmaster's Council at Tabor Academy. In 2005, Peter was one of eighteen nonprofit leaders to be named Rhode Island Foundation Fellows and has embarked upon a professional and personal development program centered on studying leadership and the sail-training experience. He lives in Mattapoisett, Massachusetts, with his wife, Jennifer, his son, Luke, and his daughter, Joy.

IF YOU GO

➤ **Getting There:** Buzzards Bay is roughly 60 miles from Boston and 30 miles from Providence, Rhode Island. Both cities are served by most major carriers.

➤ **Best Time to Visit:** Summer offers the most clement weather but is also the busiest season. Early fall can be a splendid time to sail about Buzzards Bay.

➤ **Charter Operators:** There are few charter operators around Buzzards Bay, but yacht clubs such as the New Bedford Yacht Club (508-997-0762; www.nbyc.com) and the Beverly Yacht Club (508-748-0540; www.beverlyyachtclub.org) sometimes offer crewing opportunities.

➤ **Moorings:** A few options include Fairhaven Shipyard and Marina (508-996-8591) in Fairhaven and Pope's Island Marina (508-979-1456) in New Bedford.

➤ **On-Shore Accommodations:** The Southeastern Massachusetts Visitors and Convention Bureau (800-288-6263; www.bristol-county.org) lists lodgings possibilities.

DESTINATION

28

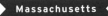
MARBLEHEAD

RECOMMENDED BY **Nick Kip**

✳

Sailing is often considered a pastime of the economically advantaged. Yet a luxurious car and a plump bank account do not give one an upper hand in making sense of the wind. This was a lesson Nick Kip learned growing up in Marblehead.

"My parents were not sailors, but they settled in Marblehead, in sight of the water," Nick explained. "It wasn't long before they had an eighteen-foot boat, and then a progression of bigger boats. There were many used boats around Marblehead, and you could get one for a reasonable price. They were living on a boat the summer I was conceived; apparently they made it to the hospital just in time for my arrival. My parents say that my first word—'bopee'—clearly meant boat.

"When I was eleven, my dad decided that living in Marblehead with sailing parents mandated that I learn to sail and race my own boat. Marblehead was blessed with some wonderful junior sailing programs, even at that time—especially the Pleon Yacht Club [*pleon* from the Greek for "sailing"]. A lot of people came into sailing around Marblehead as little kids, whether they were from blue-collar or white-collar families. Marblehead was a petri dish for young sailors. As a result, many champions and great designers evolved— George Ovay, Ted Hood, Brad Marvin, and Ray Hunt, to name a few of the greats from my childhood. I could walk down to the public park from my house in two minutes and pulley my outboard skiff into shore. My peers and I boated around more than we biked or drove. The water gave us great mobility and infinite entertainment."

Located 20 miles north of Boston, Marblehead is custom-made for boating. The quaint town, dotted with structures dating back to Revolutionary days, rests on a peninsula that extends into Massachusetts Bay, with Salem Bay sitting to the north. A neck of land juts out into the Atlantic east of the mainland, and this neck is connected to the

OPPOSITE
Whether for
commercial
fishing or
recreation,
Marblehead
has long been
synonymous
with sailing.

131

continent by a sand spit. Marblehead's deep harbor rests in the shelter formed by Marblehead Neck and the sand bar. Marblehead's first British settlers arrived in the early 1600s from Salem; the group was fed up with the Puritans' rather severe life view. By the late 1600s, Marblehead was recognized far and wide for its fishing. The fleet, which frequently plied the Grand Banks for cod, suffered a major setback in 1846, encountering a great storm on its return from the coast of Newfoundland that claimed a number of vessels. When fishing declined, Marblehead turned its seaward inclinations toward pleasure sailing.

With the popularity of sailing in Marblehead, a number of clubs sprang up to serve the populace. "In my youth, the Eastern Yacht Club (est. 1870) was the Boston Brahmin establishment, situated on the middle of Marblehead Neck, facing out on the harbor," Nick recalled. "The Boston Yacht Club (est. 1866) and the Corinthian Yacht Club (est. 1885 for smaller boat racing) were the other two big clubs. The Corinthian allowed Irish Catholics, which was not always the case at Eastern. The Marblehead Yacht Club was accepting of anyone. Though each club had its own flavor, they were not mutually exclusive—some people belonged to two or three. While people certainly had social reasons for joining the clubs, I believe that the emphasis was always on sailing. The attraction wasn't that it was a respectable thing to do. Sailing was a measure of whether you really understood the water, the tides, the breeze. It was the true test."

There's some fine cruising to be had around Marblehead. "The town is located in such a way that you can sail to many fun, sailboat-friendly places for a day," Nick continued. "Manchester-by-the-Sea is nearby, and so are Gloucester and Rockport. If you have a few more days, you can sail to Provincetown or Portsmouth, New Hampshire." But it's as a racing center that Marblehead has made its name over the last century, both hosting events and helping to create victorious sailing craft. Marblehead has been the starting or finishing port for numerous international races; national titles and Olympic trials have been determined on its waters. Since 1905, Marblehead has been the launching point for a 360-nautical-mile race across the Bay of Fundy to Halifax, Nova Scotia. The Halifax Race is held biannually, and is sponsored by the Boston Yacht Club and the Royal Nova Scotia Yacht Squadron. For many years, various members of the Boston Yacht Club contributed to the design and construction of winning America's Cup yachts.

If there's one week to soak in the ambiance of Marblehead, it would be the Marblehead Race Week, held each year at the end of July. Inaugurated in 1889, Race Week includes Junior Division, Senior One-Design and Offshore One-Design classes. "During Race Week, the harbor is absolutely jammed," Nick said. "There used to be so many boats that you could jump from boat to boat all the way across the harbor. It was the Woodstock of sailboat racing! There are parties every night. Residents sometimes host visiting yachts-people, as there simply aren't enough places to stay."

Should you make it to Marblehead during Race Week or any other time, you'll be obliged to sample a Joe Frogger, the town's unofficial sailing cookie. Dating back to Colonial times, these ginger confections were popular with fisherman because they'd keep for months at sea. The recipe has changed little in 200-plus years.

Nick Kip's mother was sailing when she was pregnant with Nick, and his family lived on a boat in Marblehead Harbor during the summers until he was five. After five years of summer camp, he stayed home in Marblehead, first learning to sail and race, then competing successfully in regional and national sailing events and teaching younger kids to sail. He even got his picture in *Sports Illustrated* in June 1960, as National Schoolboy Sailing champion. In 1962, when Nick was commodore of the Pleon Yacht Club (for juniors), someone persuaded him to take a local live-in babysitter as crew for a Saturday-afternoon race, after which a fellow sailor embarrassed him into asking the girl to a party that night. The reception after their wedding three years later was (of course) another party after the Saturday-afternoon race. He and his wife sailed in Marblehead for many years, and though both are remarried, they still live within a stone's throw of good sailing.

IF YOU GO

➤ **Getting There:** Marblehead is just 20 miles north of Boston, which is served by most major carriers.

➤ **Best Time to Visit:** Sailing is possible from mid-spring through October (or later, if you're game), but July through September is the peak season.

➤ **Charter Operators:** Atlantic Charters (781-639-0055; www.atlantic-charters.com) offers both skippered and bareboat charters.

➤ **Moorings:** Moorings are available through Northeast Mooring and Salvage (781-631-9595; www. northeastmooring.com).

➤ **On-Shore Accommodations:** The Marblehead Chamber of Commerce (781-631-2868; www.visitmarblehead.com) lists local inns and bed-and-breakfasts.

BAJA CALIFORNIA SUR

RECOMMENDED BY **Larry Pardey**

"We first visited Baja in 1968," reminisced Larry Pardey. "Lin was twenty-four and I was twenty-eight. We had a brand new boat and $5,000 in the bank—we thought we had the world! We spent several months in the area, making our living as we sailed up and down by delivering boats up to California and doing repairs. We played it like the fishing boats, staying near shore so we could duck in if a storm came up. At the time, we seemed to be the only gringos there in the summer months. We've been back several times since."

Baja California is a peninsula that extends 660 miles south from the California border. It's bounded on the east by the Sea of Cortez (or Gulf of California, depending on whom you speak to), which separates the peninsula from the rest of Mexico; to the west is the Pacific. Baja is dissected into two states: Baja California Norte (sometimes simply called Baja) and Baja California Sur. The terrain of Baja is quite mountainous, crisscrossed by four major ranges—Sierra Juarez, Sierra de San Pedro Martir, Sierra de la Giganta, and Sierra de la Laguna. The mountains serve to divert the little moisture that flows over the peninsula, rendering the region quite arid. While at times stark, Baja is a land of rich contrasts. "There is no place in the world with colors like Baja California," Larry's wife and companion, Lin Pardey, chimed in. "The contrast between the tropical greens, the turquoise of the sea and sky, with the jet black of the mountains and the pink and gold sands is absolutely startling. I've never seen anything like it."

Baja Sur, rich in both minerals and unspoiled beaches, attracts the lion's share of the peninsula's nautically minded visitors. Winter sun-seekers flock to the rather American-ized resort towns of Cabo San Lucas and San Jose del Cabo. But there are many off-the-beaten-path hideaways that await the slightly more adventurous cruiser between Loreto and the capital city of La Paz. "It's amazing," Larry continued. "In many places around

OPPOSITE
Baja Sur is a
land of stark
contrasts; the
collision of colors
is startling.

Baja—once you get away from the Americans—you have a distinct feeling that you're exploring a frontier area. The people you meet seem to be waiting to invite you into their homes. The fishermen of Baja are hardworking men, but are extremely friendly and willing to speak to anyone who anchors nearby. When we stayed in a particular area for a few weeks, we really got to know the local people. For instance, we became acquainted with a fellow who owned a restaurant in one of the little villages; before we left, we were invited to his child's wedding! A big part of the adventure has to do with the friendly people you encounter. You're only three or four hundred miles from the U.S.A., but you're in another world."

It's little wonder that this region of Baja California has caught the cruiser's fancy. The Sea of Cortez is incredibly rich in marine life—one can easily fish for grouper or dorado, swim with dolphins, and float among wintering gray whales (January through April) in the same day. Plentiful snorkeling and diving opportunities are also available. "I remember one occasion when we were anchored off the island of San Marcos, and Larry went skin-diving," Lin recalled. "He came out quicker than I expected. I asked why, and he said he'd found himself in a school of grouper. I said 'So?' He replied, 'I was the smallest in the group!'" Hikers will find abundant trails in the mountains that are never far from the sea. And those seeking a shot of urban excitement will find La Paz appealing. "It's the real Mexico, Mexico fifty years ago," Larry said enthusiastically.

One place that caught Larry's interest is Santa Rosalia, near the northern border of Baja Sur, on the Sea of Cortez. "There was a neat breakwater there," Larry continued. "We'd run to it if we hit rough weather." Santa Rosalia is sometimes referred to as "the city of wood," this owing to the wooden, French-inspired architecture that marks many neighborhoods (wood is not a common building material in this adobe-oriented part of the world). The wooden homes came compliments of a French mining company named El Boleo, which exploited the region's rich copper deposits—and for that matter, its people—for some fifty years, beginning in 1885. In addition to its incongruous wooden structures, Santa Rosalia is home to Santa Barbara, a metal church dating back to the early 1890s. "It's quite a magnificent structure," Larry commented. "With the dry climate, it hasn't rusted at all." Plaques on the church credit its design to Gustave Eiffel (of tower fame), though some architectural historians have their doubts, claiming that every building of metal fabrication from the 1880s and 1890s is credited to Eiffel.

Wandering inland from town, Larry and Lin found another interesting adventure—taking in some of the revered cave paintings of La Trinidad. "We left our boat in Santa Rosalia and took a truck into the mountains," Larry recounted. "From there, we rented a mule to take us the rest of the way." The rock art in the central Baja mountains is on par with the famous murals in southern France. The paintings have been designated a UNESCO World Heritage Site.

Anyone who's plied the waters of the Sea of Cortez has likely encountered the Coromuel wind, a dependable breeze endemic to the La Paz area. The Coromuel is a south-to-southwest wind that generally begins late in the afternoon and blows through the night; it's triggered by cool Pacific air that sweeps across the desert through a break in Baja's mountains to the warmer environs on the eastern side of the peninsula. "It seems as if this wind were designed for sailors," Lin said.

If you're going to find yourself off the grid as often as Larry and Lin Pardey, you'd do well to pick up a few first-aid tips. Sometimes that knowledge can make a difference to someone off the boat, as Larry recalled. "We were anchored in lovely Agua Verde Cove, and a Mexican gentleman rowed out to our boat in a canoe with his son. The boy had a spine in his foot, and was in great pain. Knowing we were gringos, the father assumed that we must know something about medicine. My father had been a butcher, but aside from a basic understanding about cutting flesh, I had very limited medical wisdom. We did have a book called *The Wilderness Doctor*, however, and the boy's symptoms—a swollen foot, with red streaks extending up his leg—suggested blood poisoning. Following the instructions in the book, I lanced the boy's heel so some of the blood could drain out, and then soaked his foot in hot salt water. Fortunately, the boy slowly recovered.

"For the rest of the summer, the local fishermen would come by our boat with fish and ice, calling out 'That's for Lupe!' after depositing their gifts."

Larry Pardey was born in Victoria, Canada; his first boat was an Indian dugout canoe at age nine. He met his wife-to-be, Lin, in 1965, and since that time, they've sailed hundreds of thousands of miles together around the world. Their many books include *Storm Tactics Handbook; Cruising in Seraffyn; Seraffyn's European Adventure; Seraffyn's Mediterranean Adventure; Seraffyn's Oriental Adventure; The Self-sufficient Sailor; The Capable Cruiser; The Care and Feeding of Sailing Crew; Details of Classic Boat Construction: The Hull;* and

Cost Conscious Cruiser. Lin and Larry's DVDs include *Storm Tactics, Get Ready to Cruise,* and *Get Ready to Cross Oceans.* Their articles have appeared in countless periodicals, including *Sail, Cruising World,* and *Woodenboat.* You can read their newsletters at www.landlpardey.com. Lin and Larry have also received many honors, including the International Oceanic Award presented by the Royal Institute of Navigation; the Ocean Cruising Club Award, for contributions to seamanship for small-boat sailing; the Ocean Cruising Club Merit Award, for inspiring voyages including a west-about rounding of Cape Horn; and the Seven Seas Cruising Club Service Award, for their lifetime voyaging achievements. Lin and Larry were inducted into the Cruising World Hall of Fame in 2000.

IF YOU GO

➤ **Getting There:** Aero Mexico (800-237-6639; www.aeromexico.com) offers daily flights to La Paz from a number of U.S. cities. Another option is to fly to Cabo San Lucas (served by Alaska, America West, or Mexicana Airlines) and take a bus up to La Paz (roughly four hours).

➤ **Best Time to Visit:** Baja California Sur—especially on the Sea of Cortez—is quite dry the year round. Winters are warm, summers are hot (the farther north you go, the warmer it gets). Most Americans arrive here in the winter, though the Pardeys enjoyed a summer here.

➤ **Charter Operators:** There are many small bareboat charter operators in Baja. One of the larger operators is The Moorings (888-952-8420; www.moorings.com).

➤ **Moorings:** La Paz has the most extensive yachting facilities in the central region of Baja California Sur on the Sea of Cortez. It offers a number of marinas/mooring facilities, including Marina de La Paz (+52 612 122 1646; www.marinadelapaz.com).

➤ **On-Shore Accommodations:** Loreto and La Paz are the two primary towns on the east coast of Baja California Sur. An overview of accommodations here is available at MexReservations.com (www.mexreservations.com).

NEW YORK HARBOR

RECOMMENDED BY **Billy Black**

✴

Photographer Billy Black spent the early days of his career on the island of Manhattan. It was several years, however, before he took to the waters off Manhattan.

"I started my photographic career living and working in Manhattan, and though my father and I bought an Ericson 39, we sailed it mostly on Long Island Sound. After my studio was robbed in 1981, I gave up on living in New York, and my boat and I eventually pushed on to Rhode Island. My first opportunity to sail in Manhattan came in 1987. A friend of mine, Michael Fortenbaugh, launched the Manhattan Yacht Club [now the Manhattan Sailing Club] to bring sailing to an urban population who either couldn't afford boats or didn't want the trouble of owning them. Michael was always looking for support boats for regattas, and one time I brought my boat down from Rhode Island to act as a committee boat for one of Michael's regattas. After the regatta, heading home, I found myself sailing up the East River without an engine. I'll never forget being under full sail on a starboard tack with a big Genoa. I was attempting to sail through Hell Gate, under the Throgs Neck Bridge, and I went nowhere for an hour. More than once I thought the boat would go sideways and we'd eat it, but the tide finally turned and we made it home."

The exact area that's defined by New York Harbor is the object of some debate. Some see it as the region below and around the southern tip of Manhattan. Others include these waters and extend the boundaries down to Gravesend Bay, southwest of Brooklyn. Still others use the term more generously to take in the sundry waterways that touch the five boroughs, including the lower stretches of the Hudson River, the East River, the Harlem River, Jamaica Bay, Raritan Bay, and the southwesternmost sections of the Long Island Sound. New York–based angling writer Peter Kaminsky has estimated that there are more

than 1,260 miles of coastline around greater New York—crags, crooks, and crannies included. Not all of these waters are inviting for sailors, but many are; Sail America claims that if you were to draw a 50-mile circle around Battery Park, you'd encircle a region with the highest number of registered sailboat owners in the country.

There are many sailboat clubs scattered around the five boroughs, with a nice concentration of clubs near South Street Seaport and Chelsea Piers. To find the mother of all yacht clubs, however, you must move a few blocks away from the harbor proper to the headquarters of New York Yacht Club, one of Manhattan's great contributions to the world of yachting. The club was started one June afternoon in 1844 on the deck of John Cox Stevens' new yacht *Gimcrack*, which was anchored off Battery Park. After forming the club for the purpose of "weekend New York Harbor racing, and summer cruises in the cooler New England waters," Stevens and his eight accomplices made plans to gather three days later and cruise to Newport, Rhode Island. They did so, and the waters around Newport have been a significant sailing ground for club members ever since. Suffice it to say, the NYYC has been responsible for instituting a few races in its time, including the Annual Regatta, the Atlantic Challenge Cup, and a little event called the America's Cup. Should you find yourself in midtown Manhattan, scan your little black book (or Black-Berry) for someone who knows someone who is among the club's three thousand members. The NYYC's beautiful Beaux Arts clubhouse is home to the world's largest collection of full- and half-hull models.

The boating community in New York—like everyone else—was tremendously shaken by the events of 9/11. "Richie Wilson was in New York Harbor on the *Great American II* during that second week of September in 2001," Billy recalled. "He was ready to start a record attempt from New York to Australia. When the towers came down, he found himself on the fringe of Ground Zero and postponed his departure to pitch in. A week later he rescheduled his departure and called me to come take the pictures. All the boat ramps in lower Manhattan that I'd been using for twenty years were closed. The National Guard, the Coast Guard, and the Navy were everywhere. We finally found an open ramp and launched the boat. We'd made it a hundred yards before we were pulled over and turned around by a Coast Guard boat from my home waters off Newport. Richie left without help from us and broke the record from New York to Australia.

"I was back in New York Harbor in the spring of 2006 to photograph the *Orange II*, which was preparing to break the transatlantic record. It was great to see the waterfront in

OPPOSITE The Orange II *passes in the shadow of Lady Liberty.*

DESTINATION

31

141

the middle of a big revival. Marinas were being built on the New Jersey side of the Hudson; old piers were being renovated on the Manhattan side. The New York waterfront seems to be undergoing a great resurgence.

"If I had a few hours to take someone for a sail around New York, I think I'd take them from the George Washington Bridge down to the Statue of Liberty," Billy said. "It's such an incredible transition. The Upper West Side is so very green; if you blocked out the buildings, you'd think you were in upstate New York. Traveling south, the Manhattan shoreline gets more and more urban. By the time you reach the Battery, everything is glass. On my most recent trip, we pulled the *Orange II* past the driving range at the Chelsea Piers; it was a tremendous New York moment, as not a single person stopped hitting balls to marvel at this extraordinary boat! We continued down to the Battery, and we were taking some shots with the western light—except it was being simultaneously backlit by the reflected light. It was one-of-a-kind lighting for a unique craft."

Billy Black has many memories of New York Harbor, of friends who left for adventures never to return from sea, and of the devastation that followed the 9/11 attacks. One memory that's especially poignant involves a brief sail with his wife's mother, Beverly. "My wife, Joyce, is originally from Denver, and a few years back Beverly came out to spend a little time on the East Coast," Billy recalled. "The morning after she arrived, we took our boat from the Palisades on the New Jersey coast for a sail to the city. That first view from the river of the beautiful green shoreline gave Bev an indelible and atypical impression of the city. We sailed through the waters past the old Cunard Line docks, under the bridges, and past the piers. The ultimate view on that beautiful morning was the Statue of Liberty. It felt as if we could reach up and touch it. To view a familiar landmark from a small boat on the water is an unforgettable thrill. Seeing the statue so close to Ellis Island, you can't help but feel an emotional connection with the people who came as immigrants to this huge, strange land and saw this glorious statue as we were seeing it.

"Though she always enjoys the energy, activity, pulse, and taxi horns of the city, Bev never forgets the beauty of her first view of New York from the harbor. It was a tremendous thrill for me, too."

Billy Black is based in Portsmouth, Rhode Island. He's known among his clients for his intrepid seamanship and for going the extra mile—even under the most challenging conditions—to get that important shot, and for displaying the patience and sensitivity to capture the spirit of an exotic location and its people. Billy has traveled all over the world to photograph places and the people who live and work there. He has worked for all the major boating publications, many builders, and suppliers of gear and services who help people get on the water. Billy's stock includes over half a million images, some of which are displayed at www.BillyBlack.com.

IF YOU GO

➤ **Getting There:** New York City is served by most airlines.

➤ **Best Time to Visit:** The months of May through October present the best sailing opportunities on New York Harbor.

➤ **Charter Operators:** Many companies offer day sails in Manhattan; fewer offer bareboat options. The Atlantic Yachting Association (917-291-7254; www.atlanticyachting.org) offers limited bareboat charters. The number of available yachts increases as you move toward New Jersey and Long Island Sound. The Manhattan Sailing Club (212-786-3323; www.myc.org) hosts races on weeknights and Saturdays, and may have crewing opportunities for visitors.

➤ **Moorings:** New York Harbor offers a great variety of berthing options, especially as you move away from Manhattan island. On Manhattan, some space for transient sailors is available at the West 79th Street Boat Basin 212-496-2105; www.nycgovparks.org).

➤ **On-Shore Accommodations:** The New York State Department of Tourism (800-CALL-NYS; www.iloveny.com) has a comprehensive listing of accommodations in the Big Apple.

DESTINATION

31

AUCKLAND

RECOMMENDED BY **Penny Whiting**

✳

Sailing is a way of life for many Aucklanders, and Penny Whiting's racing career began at the tender age of two. "I was born and raised here, and my father was a passionate sailor," Penny recounted. "I was the firstborn of five children, so I was my father's son for a few years, until my younger brother could join us. For certain races, he needed a two-person crew to qualify. If it was a light-wind day, he'd take me and my teddy bear along."

The Maori phrase for Auckland—*Tamaki-Makau-Rau*—translates as "the maiden with a hundred lovers." This poetically speaks to the region's many natural and cultural attractions. Auckland combines a multicultural sophistication with unspoiled natural beauty that's paralleled by few other cities. "Visitors from the United States and Europe are blown away by the clean air, the greenness, and the cleanliness of the place," Penny explained. "A queue is something people here don't understand; after all, New Zealand has only four million people in a land mass the size of California. As far as boating opportunities go, our nickname—'The City of Sails'—says it all."

And the opportunities are many, both for racers and cruisers. Auckland has hosted several recent America's Cup races, including the most recent match in 2003, in which Switzerland's Team Alinghi bested Team New Zealand, bringing the cup to Europe for the first time. The city is home to some forty yacht clubs, which all host a regular assortment of competitions.

"Auckland Harbor is sheltered and confined, which makes it different from other harbors I've sailed in," Penny continued. "It's roughly four miles long and one mile wide, and there's seldom much of a swell. The harbor is very accessible to our residents, and sailing is quite popular with New Zealanders. I think this may be because boating is generally affordable here. Some years ago, my son and two of his friends (age thirteen, fifteen, and

OPPOSITE
Bay of Islands,
north of
Auckland, offers
many secluded
spots where
cruisers can hide
away.

DESTINATION

32

145

sixteen, respectively) bought a 26-foot keelboat outfitted with all the equipment they'd need. Each of the families put in $3,000 NZ. For a modest investment, we gave these boys a lifelong hobby, an introduction to the outdoor life. My son and the other young men are now all competing in the America's Cup. I have a little theory on boating, and on life: if you want to go boating, buy a boat and go. Why put your money in a bank so other people can borrow your money and use it to buy themselves a boat?"

Just outside of Auckland Harbor rests one of the most expansive cruising areas in the world, Hauraki Gulf, which spans more than 1,500 square miles and is populated with upward of seventy islands. "The Great Barrier Island, about sixty miles off Auckland, protects the gulf most of the time from heavy seas," Penny said. "While there isn't a tremendous number of swells, there is one thing visiting cruisers must take note of: our tides rise and fall twelve feet every six hours. This can make for bumpy conditions if you're not working with the tide.

"If I'm going to go on a cruising trip, I'll choose a destination based on the amount of time we have. If I've got a couple of days, I might head to Kawau, which is about thirty nautical miles from Auckland. It has lovely deep coves, sandy beaches, and a number of good bushwalks. If I had ten days, I'd head north 120 nautical miles to Bay of Islands. This is a wonderful cruising playground, very popular with Aucklanders, especially around Christmas. New Zealanders don't celebrate Christmas with as much pomp as people in the U.S.; instead, it's simply a time to do things with your family, and our family always sailed. If I only had a day to entertain you, I might take you to Waiheke Island, which is only about twelve miles off Auckland. They make some nice wines there.

"I must mention that cruising in New Zealand is somewhat different than what I've seen of cruising in America," Penny commented. "It seems that many Americans go from marina to marina, where services such as restaurants are available. Here, once you're out, there aren't many marinas or restaurants. Basically, you find an anchorage, barbecue on your stern, or go to a friend's boat and have meals there. You don't rely on shore-based activities. Fishing can be a huge part of our boating experience. When we're under sail, we'll troll lures behind us for kingfish, or we'll pull into a little bay, dinghy over to a point, and drop a line down for silver snapper. It's also fairly easy to collect scallops, crayfish, and oysters. If you like to forage, you'll do well here."

Given its many blessings, there's never a bad time to be on Auckland Harbor. But one truly special time is the Auckland Anniversary Regatta, which is held each January 29th to commemorate the establishment of Auckland by Captain William Hobson in 1840.

"All the boats showcase themselves," Penny observed, "little boats from little yacht clubs, big boats from big yacht clubs. They're all out parading around. There are so many great vantage points around the harbor, everyone comes out to watch. The timing is perfect, as the Anniversary Regatta falls on my birthday."

Penny Whiting is best known as a yachtswoman and the owner-operator of the Penny Whiting Sailing School (www.pennywhiting.com), but she has also been a swimming champion, international surfing competitor, rugby coach, writer, celebrity speaker, mother of two, America's Cup and Whitbread commentator, and Auckland city councilor. As the eldest child in the family, she accepted responsibility from an early age, and while still in her teens she went into business with her brother Paul designing and building boats. She went on to found the Penny Whiting Sailing School. In more than thirty years she has not missed one class, and her yacht *Endless Summer*, floating school to over twenty thousand students, is a familiar sight on Auckland's Waitemata Harbor.

IF YOU GO

➤ **Getting There:** Auckland is served with direct flights from Los Angeles and California, and from a number of Asian cities. Carriers serving Auckland include Air New Zealand, Cathay Pacific, Qantas, and Singapore Airlines.

➤ **Best Time to Visit:** The New Zealand summer—December through March—provides the most clement weather, though it's warm enough to sail throughout the year.

➤ **Charter Operators:** For day trips, you can sail on an America's Cup yacht through Explore NZ (+64 9 358 3137; www.explorenz.co.nz). For bareboat yachts, contact The Moorings (888-952-8420; www.moorings.com) and Paradise Adventures & Cruises (+61 2 8799 2500; www.paradiseadventures.com.au).

➤ **Moorings:** There are eight major marinas in the city according to www.noonsite.com, including Westhaven Marina (+64 9 309 1352; www.westhaven.co.nz).

➤ **On-Shore Accommodations:** Tourism Auckland (+64 9 979 7070; www.aucklandnz. com) is a good jumping-off point for lodgings options in greater Auckland.

SPITSBERGEN

RECOMMENDED BY **Onne van der Wal**

For more than twenty years, photographer/sailor Onne van der Wal has traveled the world chronicling regattas and capturing adventures on film. Despite many harrowing journeys, he had never been beyond the Arctic Circle until he set foot on the *Shaman.*

"I accompanied the *Shaman* on an extended trip in the summer of 1996 to help document the owner's journey," Onne said. "We were off the coast of Norway, and one day the gentleman suggested that we head for Spitsbergen. It's situated at 80 degrees North, very extreme. Few people go there; over two weeks, we saw one other sailboat. As you'd imagine, it's very quiet and peaceful."

Spitsbergen is the largest island in the Svalbard archipelago, covering over 15,000 square miles. It's situated in the Arctic Ocean, some 400 miles north of the northernmost point of the Norwegian mainland and 600 miles south of the North Pole. The northernmost point in Europe, it's further north than any point in Alaska. The landmass of Spitsbergen—and the other islands in the archipelago, for that matter—is largely glaciated, and otherwise covered with snowfields and tundra. The treeless island is bifurcated by numerous deep fjords, and is also mountainous, with jagged peaks sticking out at odd angles (one peak, Newtontoppen, reaches over 5,600 feet). An interesting sidenote that speaks to Spitsbergen's isolation: the island has been chosen by the Norwegian government to house a "doomsday" seed bank where as many seeds as needed from the world's plant species will be stockpiled to prevent plants from going extinct in the event of nuclear war or gene pollution from genetically engineered plants.

The Svalbard, "cold coast" in the Norwegian language, is believed to have been first discovered in the late twelfth century by Viking explorers. After a brief appearance in an Icelandic book, it was largely forgotten until 1596, when the Dutch navigator Willem

OPPOSITE
One has the sense of being quite alone in a place like Spitsbergen.

DESTINATION

33

Barentsz came upon the archipelago. (Spitsbergen is Dutch for "jagged peaks.") During the next four centuries, various European nations took turns extracting the archipelago's resources. In the seventeenth century, the English and Dutch took whales. In the eighteenth century, Russians and Scandinavians took furs. Late in the nineteenth century, large coal deposits were discovered. This led three nations—Russia, Sweden, and Norway—to lay claim to the Svalbard. Norway was awarded possession in 1925. Today, the three most populous islands on the archipelago—Spitsbergen, Bjornoy, and Hopen—have roughly three thousand hardy souls. The largest town is Longyearbyen on Spitsbergen. Though the Svalbard belongs to Norway, nearly 70 percent of its residents are of Russian descent, drawn there to work the coal mines. (Note: Some refer to the entire archipelago as Spitsbergen; Norwegians prefer Svalbard.)

"With its glaciers and mountains, Spitsbergen is absolutely majestic," Onne commented. "During our two weeks there, we'd go ashore every day at least twice and hike for three or four hours. In July and August—the only time you can visit—you have the midnight sun. From a photographer's perspective, the light is magic—soft and golden—especially from nine p.m. to four a.m. One can be anchored in a place, and in the course of the day, you'd see the bay, mountain, and glacier lit from a 360-degree perspective. The sun would go down a bit and then move left to right. Many a time I'd be on deck at three or four a.m., even though I was quite tired from my hiking. The light was fascinating; I couldn't tear myself away." The midnight sun is with Spitsbergen from late April to late August; come late October through February, the polar night descends.

As the only significant landmass for hundreds of miles, Spitsbergen is a magnet for wildlife. Thousands of sea birds nest on the cliffs, including murres and kittiwakes and ivory gulls. While much of the land-based mammal life was decimated by hunters in the last century, Spitsbergen has several herds of Svalbard reindeer, a smaller species endemic to the archipelago. Arctic fox are also commonly encountered. The waters around Spitsbergen attract great numbers of marine mammals, including beluga and minke whales; bearded, ringed, harbor, and harp seals; and walrus.

And their great nemesis—*Ursus maritimus.*

The polar bear is one of the most fearsome predators in the world. Unlike other members of the bear family, it relies solely on meat for sustenance—especially the meat of ringed seals—though it will eat anything it can kill, including belugas . . . and men. Males can run as large as 1,700 pounds, though they average closer to 1,000 pounds; females are quite a bit smaller, averaging closer to 500 pounds. Polar bears spend most of their time patrolling the ice packs, seeking the air holes that might indicate the presence of a ringed seal. Estimates place the *Ursus maritimus* population around Spitsbergen in the vicinity of five hundred. "When walking around, you have to be extremely careful about the bears," Onne recalled. "You have to have a guy with a high-powered rifle escorting you, as the bears are hungry and aggressive." Five people have been killed by polar bears around Spitsbergen since 1973; carrying a gun is actually required by law. (Biologists estimate that there are 20,000 polar bears remaining in the Arctic, though their long-term well-being is uncertain, thanks to declining ice packs attributed to global warming.)

Through the two weeks that they were around Spitsbergen, Onne and his party used the boat as a base. "It was a decent-size craft," Onne said, "but seeing our big boat in the distance looking so small when we were on land made us realize how vulnerable we were in this beautiful but forlorn place."

Onne van der Wal has been a nautical, sailing, and yacht photographer for over twenty years. Once a professional sailor, he got his start in photography while sailing with the 1981–82 Dutch Whitbread Around the World Race Team on their winning boat, *Flyer*. When Onne returned from their winning circumnavigation, the press was eager to see the many sailing photos he had shot. These yachting photos are still published today, as they came to represent the photographic style and elements he is now well known for. Dramatic angles from the masthead or the end of the spinnaker pole are examples of the effort Onne will put into any assignment or boating photo-shoot he accepts. Onne has crossed the Atlantic more than ten times, and has raced in many other transoceanic events. Most recently his ocean sailing has been on nautical photographic expeditions, which have taken him as far north as Spitsbergen in the Norwegian Arctic and as far south as Antarctica. In the winter of 2003 Onne was fortunate enough to photograph an epic journey to retrace the steps of Sir Ernest Shackleton on the island of South Georgia in the Falkland Islands. Onne lives in Jamestown, Rhode Island, with his wife, Tenley, and their three children, Read, Billy, and Adrian, and often takes the family cruising and sailing. A gallery of his work is on display on Bannister's Wharf in downtown Newport. His first book, *Wind and Water*, was released in 2004; his award-winning sailing calendars grace the walls of countless homes.

DESTINATION

33

IF YOU GO

➤ **Getting There:** While Onne sailed from Norway to Spitsbergen, many charter sailors will opt to join their craft in Longyearbyen, the region's administrative center. Daily flights are available from Oslo (via Tromso) on SAS or Braathens.

➤ **Best Time to Visit:** There's a finite window for visiting the Arctic, from late June to mid-September.

➤ **Charter Operators:** Several companies lead sailing charters to Spitsbergen, including Adventure Associates (+61 2 8916 3000; www.adventureassociates.com) and Pelagic Sailing Expeditions (www.pelagic.co.uk).

➤ **Moorings:** Should you endeavor to venture to Spitsbergen on your own, moorings and other services are available in Longyearbyen and Ny Ålesund, which is considered the northernmost human settlement in the world.

➤ **On-Shore Accommodations:** Options are somewhat limited in Longyearbyen, though the SAS Radisson (888-201-1718; www.sasradisson.com) is one choice.

BRAS D'OR LAKE

RECOMMENDED BY **John Bryson**

In 1886, Alexander Graham Bell decided that he had earned a vacation. As he and his wife sailed north along the New England coast toward Newfoundland, they tucked into Bras d'Or (French for "arms of gold") Lake on Nova Scotia's Cape Breton Island. In some ways, he never left. Bell would go on to build a grand estate overlooking the lake in the shadow of Beinn Breagh, Scottish Gaelic for "beautiful mountain." Bell died and was buried there in 1922.

In his latter years, Dr. Bell was very interested in hydrofoil design, and with the help of Walter Pinaud, he developed the *HD4*, a boat that would set the world's marine speed record of almost 71 miles per hour. Still, he had a soft spot for sailing. In 1917, Dr. Bell had a sailboat built and named for his daughter, Elsie. "While the boat was sailed primarily on the Bras d'Or," John Bryson explained, "the captain would occasionally take it outside to other ports. It's said that Dr. Bell strictly instructed the captain not to mention the Bras d'Or to anyone who might ask him where he'd sailed from."

Fortunately for the rest of us, the good word about the Bras d'Or has snuck out!

By its very nature, Bras d'Or Lake is something of an enigma. Is it saltwater or fresh? Is it one lake or two? The answer to question one is yes—the salinity of the Bras d'Or qualifies it as brackish water, a product of the seawater that drains in from the Atlantic through two natural outlets in the northeast and one manmade connection in the southwest, and the runoff from several rivers that terminate here. It's a unique ecosystem—in some sections, cod and lobster thrive; in others, a baited hook might bring a rainbow trout to hand! Regarding question two, most oceanographers would classify the 660 square miles of the Bras d'Or as one lake, though the Washabuck Peninsula and several other landmasses have the effect of dividing the lake into numerous subregions. Cape Bretoners

generally use the plural. Salt or fresh, lake or lakes, most everyone can agree that the island that is home to the Bras d'Or, Cape Breton, is one of the world's most scenic northern islands, with rugged pine-covered mountains, verdant valleys, and views of the Atlantic, the Gulf of St. Lawrence, or the Bras d'Or just about anywhere you look.

"Bras d'Or Lake has several qualities that make for exceptional sailing," John explained. "First, it's fog-free. That may not mean much to folks in some parts of the world, but here it's a big thing. If you were to go out to the coast, from here down to Halifax, all you'd be able to see many days would be the bow of your boat. Once you sneak into St. Peter's Canal [one of the entrances to the Bras d'Or], it's all sunshine, not a drop of fog. In seventeen seasons, I can remember only two or three mornings when there was fog—and it burned off before lunch. A second great quality about the Bras d'Or is the winds—very steady, but seldom too strong. I'd say that 95 to 98 percent of the time, there's wind at some point of the day, so you seldom have to motor. Those rare days when the wind gets up to 30 or 35 knots, we won't experience seas that are more than two or three feet—we're that sheltered. With nine hundred miles of coastline around the lake, there's always a place to get out of the wind, and many wonderful places to anchor up. There's quite a bit of wildlife. You're almost sure to see bald eagles, and in out-of-the-way spots like Maskill's Cove, you might come upon a moose. Finally, there just aren't many people on the water here. On a good day in the middle of August—our high season—whether it's a Tuesday or a Saturday, if I can see three or four boats in a ten-mile radius, it's a crowded day."

Part of the allure of Bras d'Or Lake is the chance to partake of Cape Breton's thriving Celtic culture, and the genuine hospitality of the islanders. "People on the island understand the importance of tourism to Cape Breton's economy," John said. "While I think they're a friendly group to begin with, they go the extra mile to make people feel welcome." Though initially settled by the French in the early 1700s and then ceded to England in 1763, Cape Breton has been shaped most profoundly by Scottish immigrants, who arrived in the early 1800s. (Oddly enough, geologists believe that Cape Breton may have initially been connected to Scotland millions of years ago!) These Scots, forcibly displaced from the Scottish Highlands, managed to maintain much of their way of life. While the number of citizens speaking Gaelic is shrinking, the region's culture is being passionately preserved in its music, especially a style of violin playing that's been branded "Cape Breton Fiddling," characterized by such artists as Natalie MacMaster. A special time to visit Cape Breton and the Bras d'Or is October, when the Celtic Colors International

OPPOSITE
The Alexander Graham Bell estate at Beinn Breagh, on beautiful Bras d'Or Lake.

DESTINATION

34

Festival occurs, showcasing the island's musical heritage. "You can still sail comfortably into the middle of October," John added, "though it's a bit cool in the early morning and late afternoon. Still, the vibrancy of the fall colors is just out of this world. When we have visitors, I always like to sail past the Bell property at Beinn Breagh. With the right colors, it's like a picture postcard."

John Bryson was raised in Port Cartier on Quebec's northern shore. He was a young boy when his father began building the *Amoeba*, a 67-foot Staysail schooner; he helped out whenever he could and watched quite closely as the work progressed. John joined his parents on the maiden voyage, and later as they operated the *Amoeba* as a charter vessel in the U.S. Virgin Islands. He learned to sail by doing, mainly from his father, but he has sailed many other boats in the islands, raced with other boaters, and made numerous ocean crossings delivering sailboats. He has owned and operated Amoeba Sailing Tours (www.amoebasailingtours.com) in the town of Baddeck on the Bras d'Or since 1989, leading lake tours and hosting weddings, family reunions, and other special events.

▶ IF YOU GO ◀

➤ **Getting There:** The town of Baddeck is the sailing center of the Bras d'Or. Air Canada offers daily flights to Halifax, Nova Scotia, from a number of North American cities, with connecting flights to Sydney, which is on the island of Cape Breton. From Sydney, it's 50 miles to Baddeck.

➤ **Best Time to Visit:** The summer months are most reliable. Good weather can be found into October, though it can get cold quickly at that time of year.

➤ **Charter Operators:** Harvey Bareboat Charters (902-295-3318; www.baddeck.com/harvey) and Cape Breton Boat Yard (www.capebretonboatyard.com) have bareboat charters available. Several operators, including Amoeba Sailing Tours, offer day sails.

➤ **Moorings:** Berths are available from the Cape Breton Boat Yard.

➤ **On-Shore Accommodations:** Over thirty lodgings options around Baddeck are listed by the Baddeck and Area Business Tourism Association (www.visitbaddeck.com).

LAKE HURON'S NORTH CHANNEL

RECOMMENDED BY **Mark Stevens**

Lake Michigan has "The Mac." Lake Superior has the Gordon Lightfoot song "The Edmund Fitzgerald." Lake Huron has the North Channel.

"For anyone who's spent any time sailing on the Great Lakes, the North Channel is a spot to aspire to," Mark Stevens began. "It's someplace people feel they need to visit before they die. I've been in bars in faraway places like St. Maarten, chatting with other sailors. They'll ask me where my favorite place to sail is, and I'll tell them the North Channel. If they've been there, they'll get a hazy look in their eyes and tell me about their favorite anchorage."

The North Channel rests just below the northern perimeter of Lake Huron, approximately 120 miles south of Sudbury, Ontario. It's formed by Manitoulin Island to the south, the largest freshwater island in the world. Manitoulin Island stretches nearly 80 miles from east to west, and is 30 miles wide in parts; it contains more than a hundred lakes. The island and other environs in the channel are under First Nations sovereignty, and this has prevented much development from occurring around Manitoulin. One road does cross to the island on its northeastern corner, but for those traveling by car from the States or Toronto, it's a near-epic journey. Most come here by boat. "I would venture that of the three hundred islands in the channel, there are only inhabitants on thirty or forty," Mark said. "You don't see cottages or other signs of man, other than the occasional boat. There's nothing but unadulterated nature. At the same time, however, you're never more than a three-hour sail from a town."

The North Channel is ensconced in the north woods and, for Mark, captures the very essence of his homeland. "The Channel is the perfect metaphor for my vision of Canada," he explained. "A wild place with massive pink granite boulders, crippled pine trees, and

DESTINATION

35

sky-blue waters where you can see down twenty feet. To the north, you have the quartzite La Cloche Mountains. When the sun gleams off them, they look as though they're cloaked in snow. To the south, it's Manitoulin Island, a sheltering presence cloaked in greens and blues and purples as the sun plays through the sky."

"Manitoulin" translates to "island of the spirits" in the language of the Anishnaabeg people (a description used by many belonging to the Odawa, Ojibwe, and Algonquin nations). Many who have visited the island speak of a sense of history or time eternal that seems to hang in the air. Archeological records show that indigenous peoples have lived on the island for some nine thousand years. Europeans, in the form of French missionaries and fur traders, first arrived in the mid-1600s. Though later attempts at farming were unsuccessful because of poor soil conditions, loggers arrived in the late 1800s and soon the island was denuded of its original growth, though Mother Nature has replenished the forests of pine and hardwoods in admirable fashion. There are several small towns on the island. Gore Bay serves as a point of departure for many cruisers, and is an excellent place to both charter and provision a boat. On the eastern side of the island, the communities of Wikwemikong and Manitowaning maintain much of their Anishnaabeg flavor, offering a window into the life of Manitoulin's native people. Tucked in on Mudge Bay is little Kagawong, which boasts some fine examples of the limestone structures that typified early European construction here.

While it's difficult for Mark to single out one favorite place in the Channel, he would have to choose the Benjamin Islands, east of Gore Bay. "First, you push through Whales-back channel, a delightful seventeen-mile stretch that includes Beardron Harbor and John Island," Mark described. "Farther east you reach the Benjamins, North and South." Navigating around the Benjamins can be a little tricky, thanks to the presence of many small rocks. But a little careful maneuvering is well rewarded. "One morning while anchored there, we dinghied over to a 200-foot-high granite outcropping and climbed it to scan the channel, which was visible for miles from this perspective. Our boys swam from a wide ledge far below the ridge, then skipped stones across the water. A single boat headed east, its white sail standing out against the indigo hump of Manitoulin Island. Except for two other boats swinging at anchor in the same bay, we couldn't see another sign of humanity."

As you prepare to turn in at night, your craft tucked into a little granite channel and tied to a spruce on shore, Mark would encourage you to look up. "The Aurora Borealis

OPPOSITE
For Lake Huron
sailors, the
North Channel
is the holy
grail of cruising
grounds.

DESTINATION

35

provides an incredible show—shades of pink and lime and lavender dancing in the sky. Once you see it, you'll understand why the Algonquin people called the Aurora Borealis the Spirit Dance."

Mark Stevens owns a Contessa 26, which he sails on Lake Ontario. He has sailed a multitude of Caribbean Islands, but the North Channel remains the first love of this former sailing instructor. He writes for *Canadian Yachting, Powercruising, Pacific Yachting, Cruising World,* and *Sailing* on a regular basis and has also written for *Bluewater Sailing*, *Men's Fitness,* and *Sail.* His credits include *Ski Press* and *Ski Canada,* for when it's too cold to sail. He is the recipient of two Northern Lights Canadian Media Awards, the Ottawa Tourism Travel Writing Award, and the Cayman Islands Media Award for Excellence in Caribbean Travel Writing. His wife, the photographer Sharon Matthews-Stevens, received the 2005 Starwood Resorts Award for Excellence in Travel Photography.

◄ **IF YOU GO** ►

➤ **Getting There:** Gore Bay on Manitoulin Island is the main sailing hub on the North Channel. It's roughly 350 miles by car from Toronto, which is served by most major carriers. Gore Bay is about 120 miles from Sudbury, Ontario, which is served from Toronto by Air Canada.

➤ **Best Time to Visit:** May through October are the most reliable weather months; swimmers may want to time their visit for July or August.

➤ **Charter Operators:** Canadian Yacht Charters (800-565-0022; www.cynorth.com) in Gore Bay and Discovery Yacht Charters (800-268-8222; www.sailingdiscovery.com) in Little Current both offer bareboat options.

➤ **Moorings:** Berths are available at the Gore Bay Marina on Manitoulin Island (705-282-2906) and at North Channel Yacht Club (www.ncyc.ca), which is on Serpent Harbor on the mainland north of the channel.

➤ **On-Shore Accommodations:** All the available lodgings on Manitoulin Island are listed at www.manitoulin-island.com.

NEWPORT

RECOMMENDED BY **Jeff Johnstone**

✳

When the family that lent its first initial to one of the most popular brands of sailboat had to find a spot to set up shop, there was little question where to go.

"J Boats was founded in 1977 in Connecticut," Jeff Johnstone recalled, "but within twelve months the founders, Bob and Rod Johnstone, decided to move the company to Newport. From a business standpoint, it made perfect sense. The marine infrastructure was already in place, and there was a certain cachet. For sailing, it was the obvious place to be. What struck me first about Newport Harbor was that it was filled with sailboats, probably eighty percent, while most harbors are dominated by powerboats. And it hasn't changed much in the past twenty-five years. With a deep-water harbor, a large navigable bay, easy access to the ocean, and a great funneling sea breeze that draws in between Block Island to the southwest side and Martha's Vineyard to the southeast, it's no surprise that Newport's been a sailing haven since the early 1700s."

Though other ports have claimed the title of "Sailing Capital of the World," few would argue the merits of Newport's claim. The region's prominence in the sailing world followed from its selection by the rich and famous as a playground; before any sailing sobriquets had been designated, Newport was dubbed "America's First Resort." The superwealthy of the day began congregating in Newport in the 1850s, ushering in a period of social pomp and circumstance that became known as the Gilded Age; it's estimated that "The 400," a term given to describe the prosperous families that made up the social core of Newport, had by the 1870s amassed 80 percent of the wealth in America. While the relatively idle time many summer residents had in greater Newport—not to mention the region's robust fishing industry—helped contribute to the birth of a sailing mecca on the coast of southern Rhode Island, the arrival of the America's Cup race did

not hurt Newport's sailing élan. From 1930 until 1983, the race (sponsored by the New York Yacht Club, keeper of the cup for its first 131 years) was held in the waters off Newport. It was here that the Cup was wrested away from the United States by Australian Alan Bond and his *Australia II* in 1983.

Newport Harbor is part of Narragansett Bay, a section of water that's often defined by Whale Rock (off the town of Narragansett) to the southwest, the capital city of Providence to the north, and Sakonnet Point to the east. It totals nearly a hundred square miles of water. Within the bay are three significant islands: Conanicut, which is home to Jamestown and creates the West and East Passages; Aquidneck, the island where Newport, Middletown, and Portsmouth are situated; and Prudence, which rests roughly in the center of the bay. While some shoals are present around the bay's dozen smaller islands, the water tends to be deep enough to keep most sailors high and dry. "The entrances to the bay can be choppy, but once you're in, it's relatively flat water," Jeff continued. "Whether you're a seasoned sailor or not, there are plenty of places you can sail and learn to sail. On any given afternoon on Narragansett Bay you'll see hundred-year-old classics, little plastic boats, and the latest Grand Prix racers. It's truly a melting pot of boats."

Making landfall in Newport is one of sailing's great moments, especially if you enter through the East Passage when the wind is behind you. "First you come upon the Castle Hill Lighthouse to starboard, where you'll usually find a crowd having a picnic and enjoying the weather on the nearby lawns in front of the Inn at Castle Hill. The water's quite deep there, and you can sail within twenty-five feet of shore. Beavertail Light [a lighthouse dating back to 1749] is on your port side. As you continue in, there are the Hammersmith Farms estate, the Kennedy summer White House in the early 1960s, on the right and Fort Adams, a military base dating back to the 1820s [and since 1959, the site of the Newport Folk Festival]. The only thing you miss on this entrance are the mansions of the Gilded Age, most of which are on the other side of Newport.

"We like to take friends sailing—and even those who don't know much about sailing have a great time. If we had three hours on a summer afternoon, we'd head out of Newport Harbor past Fort Adams toward Castle Hill, and then bear off to the west to Mackerel Cove—and sail into Mackerel Cove over on Conanicut Island and drop anchor in about eighteen feet of water. We'd take a swim and have a bite to eat, and then we'd pull anchor and head north along the Jamestown shoreline, zip under the Newport Bridge, sail near the aircraft carriers and the Naval War College, and then duck back into the harbor.

OPPOSITE
Sailing into Newport is a rite of passage for cruisers and racers alike.

DESTINATION

36

Time permitting, we'd do a 'harbor burn'—that is, sail counterclockwise around the harbor, and see all the boats in town—everything from America's Cup 12-meters under full sail to classic wooden yachts. We're really spoiled; there aren't too many places that can offer that kind of magical experience."

While the America's Cup has been gone nearly twenty-five years, there's still a good deal of racing to be found around greater Newport. The Newport to Bermuda Race attracts some of the world's top racers biannually in June. In July, there's the Newport Regatta (sponsored by Sail Newport), which features twenty classes of one-designs, plus IRC and PHRF classes, and draws over three hundred boats. In September, there's the Classic Yacht Regatta (sponsored by the Newport-based Museum of Yachting); this race features wooden boats built before 1950, and is one of the largest races of its kind. "As a racer," Jeff added, "you can be sailing nearly every night in some kind of organized race, and chances are you'll be competing against an Olympic, America's Cup, or World Champion sailor. There's Monday night Lasers and Matchracing; Tuesday nights at Jamestown and the Newport Yacht Club; Wednesday is Shields night; Thursdays, the J/24s sail out of Ida Lewis Yacht Club. It's not unusual for visitors to find a crew spot at the last minute. All you have to do is show up at the dock with some sneakers and a sunny disposition, and you're likely to be invited."

When the racing is done, there are several spots where local sailors like to retire. "While the Black Pearl and the Clarke Cooke House are musts for any visiting sailor," Jeff said, "the locals like to hang out at Café Zelda and the AC [International Yacht and Athletic Club] on Lower Thames Street. Any night after work, you'll bump into a great sailing crowd including boat builders, designers, yacht captains. If you want something to read later in the evening, the Armchair Sailor bookstore is right across the street. And if it starts raining, stop by next door at Team One Newport to check out the latest sailing gear."

Jeff Johnstone is president of J Boats, Inc., headquartered in Newport, Rhode Island. A lifelong one-design sailor, as a teenager Jeff was part of the "work crew" that built and sailed the original J/24 *Ragtime* in 1976. After sailing at Connecticut College, Jeff co-founded the J World Sailing School in 1981 (also in Newport), and still serves on the board of directors. He was involved with the start-up of junior sailing at Sail Newport in 1984 and later served as the organization's president in 1994–95. In 1987, Jeff, along with his brother and cousins (the second-generation Johnstones), took over the management reins of J Boats. Since then, J Boats has introduced twenty-three new designs and garnered twenty-one industry awards. Jeff's recent projects include starting a junior big boat at his home club, the Ida Lewis Yacht Club. On the race course, his weapon of choice is the J/24, which he sails with his teenage daughters every Thursday night.

IF YOU GO

➤ **Getting There:** Newport is 20 miles from Providence and 60 miles from Boston, both of which are served by most major carriers.

➤ **Best Time to Visit:** Conditions are conducive to sailing from April through October. September can be a fine month to visit, as the weather is still pleasant but the crowds have thinned out.

➤ **Charter Operators:** Newport may have more charter options than any other venue in America. For an overview, contact the Newport County Convention & Visitor's Bureau (800-326-6030; www.gonewport.com). As Jeff mentioned, polite sailors will not find it terribly difficult to find a crew spot for weekday races during the summer.

➤ **Moorings:** Newport has ample resources for visiting yachtsmen and women. A few of the many options include Conanicut Marina (401-423-7157; www.conanicutmarina.com) in Jamestown and the Newport Yachting Center (800-653-DOCK, ext.3; www. newportyachtingcenter.com).

➤ **On-Shore Accommodations:** The Newport County Convention & Visitor's Bureau (800-326-6030; www.gonewport.com) provides an extensive list of Newport region lodgings options.

FIRTH OF CLYDE

RECOMMENDED BY **Sandy Taggart**

For residents of Glasgow—and for anyone desiring excellent sailing and a taste of Scotland—the Firth of Clyde and the west coast of Scotland are magic. "It seems there's an annual pilgrimage for Glaswegians to the west coast, whether it's for racing, cruising, or anchoring in solitude," Sandy Taggart began. "One of the great advantages of the region is the string of islands available. Irrespective of the ever-changing weather, one can find an anchorage. If you decide to go somewhere and the wind doesn't cooperate, you always have other equally attractive options. You can be in the hub of things, or right out on your own with few other vessels, and you have these options within an easy half or full day's passage. There's magnificent scenery in the islands and hills of the mainland. No matter where you've sailed, you'll appreciate the beauty of Scotland's west coast."

The Firth of Clyde rests west of the city of Glasgow, where the 106-mile-long River Clyde drains into the Atlantic. ("Firth" is a Scots word for "coastal waters," generally a sea bay or estuary.) The firth is bounded to the west by the Kintyre peninsula, providing shelter from the open ocean. Roughly 50 miles from north to south, the Firth of Clyde ranges from two to 25 miles in width. How far it extends to the east is open to debate, though it can be said with certainty that the Atlantic's tidal influence is felt up to the center of Glasgow. The Firth of Clyde is dotted with islands and indented with many saltwater lochs, fingers of sea that extend inland. The rugged coastline here provides a dramatic backdrop for an exploration of Scottish history and culture.

The history of the Clyde is in many respects the modern history of Scotland. It was here that the Irish Scotti (forebears of the Scots) arrived from Ireland at the new millennium as the influence of the Romans waned. It was also here that Christianity was brought to Scotland, first by the missionary St. Ninian, near the end of the fourth century A.D., and later by St. Oran and St. Columba, in the sixth century. Much of the region's past is preserved, be it in the form of ancient stone dwellings or standing stones like Stonehenge. "We have many relics from early Celtic and Christian culture, some going back millennia, preserved on the islands of the Clyde," Sandy explained. "The Garvellochs—situated to the west of the Kintyre peninsula—have many well-maintained old dwellings, with ancient Celtic crosses. You can wander through them at will." On the island of Aran, there are countless stone circles and standing stones, some dating back to 1800 B.C., with the finest collection found at Machrie Moor.

Glasgow and environs have a rich maritime history. During the city's industrial heyday in the mid-nineteenth and early twentieth centuries, it was one of the world's largest shipbuilders, with a focus on steam-powered craft. Several factors contributed to Glasgow's predominance: the availability of large deposits of coal and iron ore in the vicinity, the presence of farsighted inventors (like James Watt) who introduced innovations to the large-scale manufacturing process, and the Clyde itself, constantly dredged to accommodate the increasingly large ships that Glaswegians were creating. It's estimated that some 30,000 ships were built in Glasgow during this golden era, including the *Queen Mary*, the *Queen Elizabeth,* and the *Lusitania.* The decline of shipbuilding brought hard times to Glasgow, casting a shadow on what was once called "the second city of the Empire." In recent years, however, Glaswegians have cannily re-created their city as a center of finance, and, with investments in their cultural heritage, as a tourist destination. Another golden era seems to hover on the horizon.

No cruise of the Clyde and western Scotland is quite complete without a visit to at least one castle, and the enjoyment of a wee dram of whisky. To fulfill the castle criterion, consider a trip to the Isle of Bute, where you'll find the Rothesay Castle. This fortification, which is unique for Scotland in its circular design, dates back eight hundred years, and was built by ancestors of the Stuart line. Rothesay survived onslaughts from Viking hordes and English forces under Cromwell before falling and being destroyed by a fellow countryman, the Duke or Argyll, in 1685. Much of the castle has been restored in the last century. Approaching the Isle of Bute through the Kyles of Bute, a narrow passage between the mainland of Argyll and Bute's north end, promises some excellent cruising.

As for whisky, connoisseurs of fine single malts could do much worse than pausing at the beautiful island of Islay, which rests just north of the Firth of Clyde, at the very beginning of the Inner Hebrides. Production of whisky dates back 200 years here, and today, seven distilleries carry on the island's fine tradition. These include Ardbeg, Lagavulin, and Laphroaig (on the south side of the island) and Bowmore, Bruichladdich, Bunnahabhain, and Caol Ila (on the north side). The south-side malts—particularly Ardbeg and Laphroaig—are renowned for their strong peat character. The Talisker distillery, on the Isle of Skye, also produces a fine whisky.

"Weather and time permitting, some more adventurous souls will sail to Lewis and Harris island," Sandy added. "You'll be alone with the seals and the deer up there. Should you make that trip, I advise you to bring some good company, and lots of good whisky."

Sandy Taggart has sailed in Scottish waters for over 50 years. He has also raced and cruised in many parts of Europe, and from time to time has participated in races to Bermuda and on Lake Michigan. A practicing chartered accountant by profession, he has used his non-sailing leisure time over the years to participate in yachting administration and to assist sail-training organizations involving youths and people with disabilities. He has been recognized for his services by a number of clubs in Britain and Ireland and by the Royal Yachting Association, the national authority in the United Kingdom. His wife, Christine, and their two daughters are also sailors; while the more energetic of the group still race on occasion, cruising is an activity enjoyed by all.

IF YOU GO

➤ **Getting There:** The city of Glasgow is served by many carriers, including American, Continental, Delta, and FlyGlobespan (a Scottish airline).

➤ **Best Time to Visit:** May through August tends to have the most sunshine and warmest temperatures, though hardy Scots certainly sail well into the fall.

➤ **Charter Operators:** Sunsail (888-350-3568; www.sunsail.com), which operates from Largs, and Alba Sailing (+44 1631 565630; www: alba-sailing.co.uk) and Portway Yacht Charters (+44 1369 820120; www.portwayyachtcharters.com), which operate from Argyll, offer bareboat charters.

➤ **Moorings:** Sail Scotland (www.sailscotland.org) reports that the Firth of Clyde has a dozen mooring/marina spots, including Largs Yacht Haven (+44 1475 675333).

➤ **On-Shore Accommodations:** Scotland's National Tourism Board (+44 845 22 55 121; www.visitscotland.com) can provide a list of accommodations.

THE SEYCHELLES

RECOMMENDED BY **Penelope Kellie**

Cruising sailors are forever searching for their next paradise, their next Garden of Eden. Some—including Penelope Kellie—believe they have found it in the Seychelles.

"I first visited the Seychelles some years back, when I was moving back to the U.K. from Asia," Penelope offered. "I spent a few days there to break up the flight, and was struck by the islands' beauty, and by the fact that they really had not yet been discovered; I saw it then as an up-and-coming destination. A few years later I visited again, this time on a boat called the *High Aspect*. While a few commercial charters were there, it was still unspoiled. And from what I understand, it still is."

The Seychelles are an archipelago of 115 islands in the Indian Ocean, roughly 1,000 miles off the coast of Kenya, and 600 miles north of Madagascar . . . which is to say, not particularly close to anywhere. This explains why the islands went undiscovered until the early 1500s, when Portuguese explorers briefly landed here. Although occasional ships stopped by to harvest turtle meat, no settlement occurred here until the mid-1700s, when the French established some control over the islands; they were named for the French finance minister at the time, Jean Moreau de Seychelles. Over the next fifty years, England wrangled with France for control of the islands, finally gaining possession in 1814. In 1976, the Republic of Seychelles gained its independence. Historically, the islands' inhabitants relied on cotton cultivation, whaling, coconut plantations, and the export of guano for economic sustenance. Since independence, the government has set aside nearly half of the total area of the islands as nature reserve or parks, recognizing both the inherent value of these resources and their potential for tourism.

Far from any mainland and riding the equator, the Seychelles present as idyllic a tropical environment as one might imagine. The air temperature hovers around 85 degrees the

DESTINATION

38

year round; the water temperature is the same. The water is incredibly clear, and its turquoise tones are offset by the white, white sand and swaying palm trees. Still, one can find beaches *almost* as nice thousands of miles closer. What brings intrepid cruisers here is the tremendous abundance of rare flora and fauna, both above the waves and below . . . and the chance to experience it with few (if any) other visitors around.

The Seychelles are a birder's paradise, boasting twelve endemic bird species, which include the Seychelles magpie robin, the Seychelles warbler, the Seychelles flycatcher, and the Scops owl. The islands—particularly Bird, Cousin, Aldabra, and Aride—are home to some of the world's most prolific seabird colonies, which include vast populations of frigatebirds, sooty terns, and noddies. Below the waves, over 1,000 species of fish have been documented, making the Seychelles a premium diving/snorkeling venue. The archipelago's seventy-four coral atolls provide a rich habitat for reef fish. When the tide comes in or goes out, larger pelagic fishes—sharks, tuna, and the like—gather near the mouths of the atoll's lagoons to ambush prey, allowing you to take in these deep-water species close to shore. (If you enjoy your fish on the end of your line, the Seychelles offer some of the finest saltwater fly fishing anywhere for bonefish, trevally, and milkfish.)

If the Seychelles have a totem species, it would be the Aldabra giant tortoise. "Giant" is not an exaggeration; male tortoises regularly grow to over 500 pounds, and the largest tortoise on record weighed in at nearly 800 pounds. These creatures also have a gigantic life span; an Aldabra giant tortoise residing in the Kolkata (i.e., Calcutta) Zoo is reputed to have lived some 255 years! The reptiles take their name from the island of Aldabra, which is located near the bottom of the archipelago. While the tortoises are strong swimmers and have appeared on other islands in the archipelago, a population of over 150,000 calls Aldabra home—rather staggering, considering that the four adjacent islands that make up Aldabra comprise just 60 square miles. Travelers making the multiday sail south from Mahé face the prospect of confronting a herd of giant tortoises, moving slowly upon the grasslands where they often feed.

While the tortoise of Aldabra may be out of reach for sailors with only a week or two to explore, another Seychelles jewel, the island of Praslin, is just twenty-five miles northeast of Mahé. Although it has its share of exquisite beaches, Praslin is most prized for the Vallée de Mai, a palm forest that continues to exist in a near-natural state in a valley near the center of the island. The valley is home to the *coco de mer* palm, producer of the world's largest seed. The seed or nut of the *coco de mer* can reach weights of nearly fifty pounds, and contains two lobes; the shape of the lobes speaks to the plant's Latin name *Lodoicea callypige*—"callipyge" is Greek for "beautiful buttocks." The seeds of the *coco de mer* attempt to expand their range through ocean dispersal. Until their source was discovered in the 1760s, some sailors believed that they grew on a magical tree on the ocean floor (presumably tended by mermaids with similarly well-appointed posteriors). Vallée de Mai is also home to a number of rare birds, including a subspecies of black parrot (*Coracopsis nigra barklyi*) that's found only on Praslin. Both Vallée de Mai and Aldabra are UNESCO World Heritage Sites. And some, incidentally, believe that the Vallée de Mai is the site of the Biblical Garden of Eden.

Penelope Kellie has worked for over twenty years in the international travel business, from offices in the Far East and in South and East Africa. In 1990, she started Penelope Kellie World Wide Yacht Charters and Tours (www.pkworldwide.com), which specializes in the management and charter of luxury yachts of all ages and sizes in venues around the world. Penelope is based on the south coast of England, near the Solent.

▸ IF YOU GO ◂

➤ **Getting There:** Mahé, the principal island of the Seychelles, is served from various European gateway cities via Air Seychelles, British Airways, and KLM/Kenya Airways.

➤ **Best Time to Visit:** The Seychelles enjoy a constant pleasant temperature and steady, predictable winds; December through February have some rain.

➤ **Charter Operators:** SunSail (888-350-3568; www.sunsail.com) and The Moorings (888-952-8420; www.moorings.com) offer bareboat charters.

➤ **Moorings:** Options include the Seychelles Yacht Club (+248 32 23 62) and the Wharf Hotel & Marina (+248 67 07 00).

➤ **On-Shore Accommodations:** Lodgings on the island of Mahé (where charter operations are based) are available from the Seychelles Tourism Board (+248 67 13 00; www.seychelles.com).

CAPE TOWN

RECOMMENDED BY **Miles Osler**

✳

The folktale goes that the *Flying Dutchman*—a ghost ship manned by a crew of damned seamen—is destined to sail the waters off the Cape of Good Hope forever, without ever rounding the headland. As far as Miles Osler is concerned, this ghoulish group of sailors has displayed exceedingly good judgment.

"We get many visitors from Europe and North America who are curious to sail here," Miles said. "After people have had a taste of the waters around Cape Town, they feel that their time sailing is one of the best things they experience over an extended trip to South Africa. I've heard that the explorer Vasco da Gama spoke of the Cape of Good Hope as the 'fairest cape he had ever seen.' That comment is special to me."

Cape Town, South Africa's third-largest city with a population approaching three million, is situated 20 miles from the Cape of Good Hope, and is one of the southernmost points on the African continent; the most southern point is actually at Cape Ahulhas, some ninety miles southeast. The cape was first viewed by European eyes in 1486, when the Portuguese explorer Bartolomeu Dias rounded the continent in search of a passage to India and the Far East; da Gama passed on the same mission a few years later. (Dias first dubbed this southern tip of Africa the "Cabo das Tormentas" or Cape of Storms; in a bit of spin control, Portugal's ruler, King John II, renamed it the Cape of Good Hope, capturing the hope for prosperity that a trade route to the East represented). The cape was not settled by Europeans until the 1650s, when the Dutch East India Company established a supply station on Table Bay, in current Cape Town proper. Over the next 250 years, possession of the cape bounced back and forth between the Dutch and the English; the Hottentot people, who are believed to have lived in the region for some 30,000 years, were rapidly displaced in the process. After the second Boer War (or Anglo-Boer War), Cape

DESTINATION

39

Town and South Africa were placed under the Union of South Africa; the country gained independence from Great Britain in 1960.

The waters around Cape Town are framed by Table Mountain, a magnificent elevation that rises over 3,500 feet above sea level from a point just a few miles north of the bay. The main face of the mesa is nearly two miles wide. "Table Mountain is just a massive, amazing sight," Miles said. "Though it's a bit back from the sea, you feel as though you're sailing at the foot of the mountain. If you're on the mountain itself, you have the chance to peer out at the bottom of Africa." Table Mountain has been designated a national park, and it's a favorite stop for visitors and local hikers alike. A cable car can take those not inclined to hike to the top of the mountain; though lions and leopards once wandered its environs, they have long since been eliminated. (Cape Town, however, is just a day's drive to areas of South Africa where visitors have an excellent opportunity to view the Big Five—lion, leopard, elephant, buffalo, and rhino.)

Off the water, Cape Town is a delight. "It's a wonderfully diverse city, very cosmopolitan," Miles observed. "I think that some expect a very Third World experience here, it being Africa and all, but Cape Town is very much a first-world city. I spent some time in San Francisco at one point in my life, and I have to say that there's a great deal of similarity between the two cities. Both are sophisticated, but well ensconced in their natural surroundings. The Victoria and Alfred waterfront—V&A, as Cape Towners call it—is very popular with visitors, somewhat like Fisherman's Wharf in San Francisco. We also have our own wine country set amongst rolling mountains—the Winelands—which has become quite popular with visitors, like Napa Valley is for San Francisco travelers."

South Africa is celebrated for its beaches, and Cape Town can claim some fine ones, including Clifton, Landudno, and Boulders Beach; the latter provides a sanctuary for African penguins. One should be forewarned that the swimming experience can vary quite dramatically from one beach to another, depending upon its location. "One of the amazing things about cruising around Cape Town is that you can sail in two oceans in one day," Miles continued. "Leaving the V&A docks in the Atlantic, we can sail around Cape Point, where we enter the Indian Ocean. On the Atlantic side, the water is fairly cool, thanks to the Beguela current; when you get to the eastern side of Cape Point, the warm Agulhus current raises the water temperature dramatically. It can take eight to sixteen hours to do the round trip, but it's a unique experience to sail two oceans in one day."

OPPOSITE Monolithic Table Mountain presides over Cape Town and the waters off the Cape of Good Hope.

DESTINATION

39

The indignity and cruelty of apartheid hang sorrowfully over South African history, though the country has made great strides in the last decade toward rectifying the injustices of the past. A powerful symbol of this dark period rests six miles off Table Bay. "Sometimes, we'll take visitors out to Robben Island," Miles said. "This is where Nelson Mandela was imprisoned." Robben Island has served as a penal colony or place of banishment for nearly four hundred years, and was infamous for its brutality during the apartheid era. For some—like Mandela—no brutality could break the power of the human spirit. "I feel—and I believe that the vast majority of South Africans feel—that Nelson Mandela has been a great unifier, a father figure for South Africa. Going out to Robben Island is still an emotional experience." Miles is not alone in his feelings.

"A few years back we had some visitors from California go out for a sail with us, and we circumnavigated Robben Island," he added. "There was an older woman amongst the group. On our return toward Cape Town, she spoke up and said that she felt her life had been fulfilled after seeing the place where Nelson Mandela had been incarcerated."

Miles Osler is co-owner of Sailactive (www.sailactive.com), a yachting company that offers private and corporate clients a unique South African interactive sailing experience. A native of South Africa, Miles has sailed in the U.K., Europe, Turkey, Thailand, Malaysia, Indonesia, Australia, Taiwan, the U.S., and Central America.

◄ IF YOU GO ►

➤ **Getting There:** Many carriers serve Cape Town, including American Airlines, British Airways, South African Airways, and United Airlines.

➤ **Best Time to Visit:** November to February is perhaps the most popular time for visitors to Cape Town, though shoulder months on either side can be quite pleasant too.

➤ **Charter Operators:** A number of operators offer day cruises, including Miles Osler's company, Sailactive (+27 21 425 6096; www.sailactive.com).

➤ **Moorings:** Moorings are available from V&A Yacht Marina (+27 21 408 7832; www.waterfront.co.za) and Royal Cape Yacht Club (+27 21 421 1354; www.rcyc.co.za).

➤ **On-Shore Accommodations:** Cape Town Routes Unlimited (+27 21 426 5639; www.tourismCapeTown.co.za) has listings for accommodations around Cape Town.

STOCKHOLM ARCHIPELAGO

RECOMMENDED BY **Thomas Rapp**

Residents of the island-city of Stockholm can claim at least 26,000 reasons why their region of the Baltic Sea is a special place to sail.

"I am a bit biased as I was brought up here, but I believe that the archipelago is the most beautiful sailing area in the world," said Thomas Rapp. "Close to the mainland there are big islands with many trees and narrow sounds. The farther out you go, the smaller the islands get. The trees begin to shrink. In the outer archipelago there are no trees at all, and the islands are only a few meters high. Imagine landscape where you can stand on a cliff and see a thousand islands, with rocks polished to an incredible luster. It's something very special—you can really feel the force of nature at work."

The Stockholm Archipelago stretches 50 miles east of the city, and encompasses some 26,000 islands, mostly resting off the coast of the provinces of Södermanland and Uppland. The islands of the archipelago are quite young, as Thomas explained. "About ten thousand years ago the inland ice receded and the ground, which for thousands of years had been pressed down by the heavy masses of ice, began to rise. None of the islands were even visible until four thousand years ago. Even today, the land continues to rise at the rate of two to four millimeters a year. The rocks were pressed together and polished as the ice moved southward, smoothing the northern part of every island like velvet; on the southern sections of the islands, the rocks are more rugged." Historically, the larger islands of the Stockholm Archipelago were thinly populated by fishermen. With the advent of steamship travel in the 1830s, the islands were made more accessible and some of Stockholm's more prosperous residents began building vacation homes on the closer islands, like Vaxholm. Today, there are some 75,000 cottages on the islands of the archipelago—though thousands of islands have little or no habitation.

Stockholm itself, with a population approaching one million residents spread over fourteen islands, is the beginning of the archipelago, and a city worthy of exploration. In a Scandinavian culture that's celebrated for high standards of cleanliness, Stockholm reigns supreme; this is at least in part due to the absence of heavy industry. The city dates back to the thirteenth century, and one can get a taste of Swedish history by visiting the *Gamla Stan* (or Old Town) on the island of Stadsholmen. Here, amongst crisscrossing alleys, you'll find the Royal Palace and the Bank of Sweden, established in 1656. Those interested in maritime history will want to leave a morning or afternoon to visit the Vasa Museum on the island of Djurgården. The *Vasa*, an ornately carved warship over 200 feet in length that was built to thwart the Swedes' eternal enemies, the Poles, set sail in August of 1628. Within minutes of its launch, the ship mysteriously sank. In 1961 it was salvaged from the ocean floor and has since been lovingly restored.

As one might imagine, with 26,000 islands to choose from, the Stockholm Archipelago offers great cruising variety. "I divide the islands into three categories," Thomas continued. "First, there are the bigger islands that have restaurants and shops and residents. These tend to be closer to Stockholm. Second, there are secluded islands where you can find a small, sheltered bay to moor your boat, put out your grill, and watch the sunset as you cook your fish or steak. Last, there are the very outer islands of the archipelago. They are very beautiful for exploring, but there's very little shelter, so these make good day-trip stops, but not good overnight places. Depending on what kind of experience people are looking for, it's pretty easy to assemble an itinerary. Even the outer islands are not that far away. Though the winds tend to be very manageable, the water is shallow and rocky. To avoid mistakes, you have to know how to read your charts. Thankfully, the availability of GPS systems makes the area quite accessible to people who are less keen on navigation."

Of the inner, more populated islands, two favorites are Sandhamn and Utö. Sandhamn (or Sand Island) is a center of sailboat racing on the archipelago and, as its name implies, has a number of beaches (Trouville is the largest and most popular). It's the launching point of the Round Götaland Race, a contest that dates back to 1937. In its current incarnation, the Round Götaland has a 500-nautical-mile course that heads south to circumnavigate the island of Götaland (the Baltic's largest island) before returning to Sandhamn. More than three hundred yachts competed in the event in 2006. Utö is a bit quieter than Sandhamn but has several restaurants, and enough high ground to offer some superb vistas of the archipelago.

Thomas is especially fond of Stora Nassa, toward the outer edge of the archipelago. "Stora Nassa is a small archipelago of its own, with hundreds of islets," Thomas explained. "That's how many of the outer islands are; there will be a cluster of many small islands, then a broad expanse of sea. Some of the islands here are forested, some are barren. One can find a spot to moor at this location, and the sunsets are just tremendous—you're given a red, red sky." Whatever island you linger upon in the Stockholm Archipelago, odds are very good that conditions will be pristine. "The city of Stockholm supports an organization that restores and maintains the public parts of the archipelago," Thomas said. "Each island has a caretaker. They maintain outhouses, provide garbage cans, and even oversee herds of sheep on some of the islands to control vegetation growth."

Thomas Rapp is the managing director of Stockholm Yacht Charter (www.sycharter.com), which provides corporate and individualized sailing tours on the Stockholm Archipelago on crewed yachts.

IF YOU GO

➤ **Getting There:** Stockholm is served by many international airlines with connections from the United States, including Air France, American Airlines, Lufthansa, and SAS.
➤ **Best Time to Visit:** From late spring to early fall, you'll find comfortable temperatures and a great deal of daylight on the Stockholm Archipelago.
➤ **Charter Operators:** SailMarine (+46 8 240 230; www.sailmarine.com) and The Moorings (888-952-8420; www.moorings.com) offer bareboat charters. Several offer skippered and day charters, including Thomas Rapp's company, Stockholm Yacht Charter (+46 8 571 67 130; www.sycharter.com).
➤ **Moorings:** Moorings are plentiful. Owned by the Swedish Cruising Club, they may be used by foreign visitors.
➤ **On-Shore Accommodations:** The Stockholm Visitor's Board (+46 8 508 28 508; www.stockholmtown.com) has listings for over 300 properties in this wonderful city.

DESTINATION

40

ANDAMAN SEA

RECOMMENDED BY **Herb McCormick**

✶

It's fair to say that Herb McCormick is taken with Thailand. "I waited a long time to visit," he said, "but having gone, I feel a tremendous desire to return. The weather is great, the people are wonderful, the food and scenery are exquisite, and everything is terrifically inexpensive, especially by Western standards. While the western coast of Thailand and the Andaman Sea are becoming more of a destination for round-the-world sailors, it's still relatively undiscovered by visiting cruisers. You never feel crowded. In fact, you often feel like you're the only visitor there."

Most adventures to the Andaman Sea begin on the island of Phuket, long a popular retreat for Thai mainlanders, and increasingly a destination for other Asian vacationers. While Phuket has some tourist trappings, once you're on the water, there's little question that you're someplace very different from Newport or Maine. "Fishermen are out with long-tail boats with high prows," Herb recalled. "The scene invokes Asia." From the port of Phuket, which is on the southern end of the island, cruisers can find memorable sailing going either north or south. To the north rests the Ao Phang-Nga National Park, a marine preserve of 150 square miles. Phang-Nga is home to 120 otherwordly islands—remnants of an ancient mountain range that was long ago flooded by the sea. "The islands have these craggy limestone peaks, like huge exclamation points," Herb continued. "You look around and feel like you're sailing into a Peter Jackson set; I half expected a winged dinosaur to fly out from behind a peak and inspect our boat." Many of the islands have *hong*s (Thai for "rooms") or caves, which can be entered by small boat via tunnels. The *hong*s are festooned with stalagmites and stalactites; one, on Panak Island, has a small, stepped waterfall. Fans of 007 will want to visit the small island of Khao Ping Gan; in the island's small bay is an even-more-diminutive island, Khao Tapoo, or James Bond Island, a jutting

DESTINATION

41

rock with no shore and a wide, flat top. It was here in 1974 that segments of *The Man with the Golden Gun* were filmed.

"One of the most awe-inspiring things I experienced in the waters of Ao Phang-Nga was the great level of phosphorescence," Herb added. "If you dive in the water at night, you leave a trail of light, as if you were being followed by a torpedo. When you come out of the water, you're dripping with light. The bioluminescence around Ao Phang-Nga was unlike anything I've ever seen. Between the visual wonders and quiet anchorages, you could take a boat up there for weeks."

From the untrammeled and unpopulated waters of Ao Phang-Nga National Park, Herb veered south to the Krabi Peninsula, where he found more activity, but an atmosphere that was equally inviting. "Three things come to mind when I think about the Krabi—the massages, the food, and the people," Herb said. "Most of the anchorages here have massage parlors where you can get a sensational Thai massage right on the beach. The masseuses are quite skilled and each has her own technique. The cost: about seven U.S. dollars. If you like to eat, Krabi is the place for you. You can eat like a king wherever you go, and it's incredibly cheap. Visit a high-end restaurant with three or four friends, and you're looking at about eight dollars; hit a roadside stand for a bowl of soup or a rice bowl with fish or chicken, and it's 75 cents. A room on the beach will set you back about five dollars. It's just about impossible to spend lots of money in Thailand. Lastly, you have the people. I've done a lot of traveling around the world, and the Thai people—wherever you are—are amongst the most upbeat, kind, and happy people I've ever been around. Whenever you encounter Thais hanging out, they are laughing and smiling. If you can learn a few words of Thai, you'll do great. Every engagement I had left me smiling."

The next stop on Herb McCormick's itinerary—the islands of Ko Phi Phi—combines beach-tourist ambiance and unsettled primacy. "The main island of Ko Phi Phi—Phi Phi Don—was the busiest place we visited," Herb continued, "with many restaurants, bars, dive shops, and knick-knack stores. It bore the brunt of the tsunami of 2004, but to my amazement, it was largely rebuilt. The Thai people are incredibly resourceful. I think that if we could send 100,000 Thai citizens into New Orleans, we'd have everything taken care of in six months. Ko Phi Phi is one of Thailand's diving centers. If you like sailing and diving, you won't find many better places to go."

The highlight of Herb's trip came near the end of his excursion, on the island of Koh Muk. "There is a series of islands off Krabi," Herb said. "Most have a resort or two and a couple restaurants, but it's very easy to find an anchorage to yourself, with palm trees and blue water—every sailor's dream! On Koh Muk, there's a special attraction called Tham Morakot, or the Emerald Cave. You take a dinghy to the mouth of the cave, and then swim up a tunnel a hundred yards or so at low tide. The tunnel opens up to a huge chamber, a hundred feet high and about fifty yards wide, with brilliant white sand. There's a hole in the top of the chamber that lets in sunlight; the light takes on a greenish hue as it reflects off the water. It's unlike anything I've ever seen in my life.

"We swam out of the cave near sunset. It's dark at the beginning of the tunnel, but as we swam toward the entrance, the setting sun—the light at the end of the tunnel, as it were—was visible. It was absolutely breathtaking."

Herb McCormick is the former editor of *Cruising World* and *Latitude 38*, and for three years he served as yachting correspondent for *The New York Times*. A sailor for over thirty years, he has cruised and raced to or from every continent on the planet. With over 30,000 offshore sailing miles to his credit, he's a veteran of most of the major ocean races, including Newport to Bermuda, the Bermuda One-Two, the Transpac, and the Pacific Cup. Herb now works as a freelance photojournalist out of Newport, Rhode Island.

▶ IF YOU GO ◀

➤ **Getting There:** The island of Phuket is generally the point of departure for sailors intent on cruising the Andaman Sea. U.S. visitors can reach Phuket via Bangkok on a number of carriers, including Japan, Malaysia, Northwest, and United Airlines.

➤ **Best Time to Visit:** The Andaman Sea region is warm and humid the year round. Most visitors will find November through March most comfortable.

➤ **Charter Operators:** Companies offering bareboat charters include SunSail (888-350-3568; www.sunsail.com) and Yacht Pro (+66 76 232 960; www.sailing-thailand.com).

➤ **Moorings:** Yacht Haven Marina Phuket (+66 76 206 704/5; www.yacht-haven-phuket.com) offers berths in Phuket.

➤ **On-Shore Accommodations:** Lodgings are plentiful and inexpensive along the Andaman Sea. Many options are outlined at Phuket.com (+66 76 236 550; www.phuket.com).

DESTINATION

41

HA'APAI

RECOMMENDED BY **Carl Hosticka**

✳

There's no particularly easy route to Tonga, though most would agree that the path that led Carl Hosticka there was particularly circuitous.

"I have a captain's license, as I do some charter sailing," Carl began. "Eventually I became a relief captain for a sixty-foot tugboat on the Willamette River in Oregon through a nonprofit called H20, which provides environmental education for middle-school students. This was the beginning of a fascination with old wooden boats. Through my activities with H20, I was introduced to a fellow in Cabo San Lucas in Baja, Mexico, named Mark Belvedere, who was seeking a relief captain for his 105-foot charter sailboat, which ran 'pirate'-style pleasure cruises. It sounded like rough duty, so I went to Cabo to check it out. I was curious, however, about why he needed a relief captain. It turned out that he had business—and a large boat—in Tonga, and that's where he'd be heading. It would take a few years, but I'd eventually be heading there too."

Until it joined the coalition of the willing in the Iraq War in 2003 (sending forty-odd troops to the conflict), many Westerners may not have heard of Tonga, let alone been able to place it on the map. Situated in the South Pacific about two-thirds of the way between Hawaii and New Zealand, Tonga consists of 169 coral atolls and volcanic islands, clustered in three main groups—Tongatapu to the south, Ha'apai in the center, and Vava'u to the north. The Tongan people have a rich seafaring history; chieftains and explorers sailing out of Tonga from 1000 A.D. to 1200 A.D. created a loosely knit empire that eventually incorporated much of Polynesia, including Fiji, Samoa, and parts of Micronesia and Melanesia. Tonga's rise to power can be credited to its navy, which relied on sailing canoes that could carry up to a hundred men. Some historians view the Tongans as the "Vikings of the South Pacific" because of their empire-building ways.

OPPOSITE
A proa plies
the waters
off Ha'apai,
in Tonga.

By the time Tonga was first visited by Europeans in the early 1600s, the empire was greatly diminished. Despite this setback, the Tongan people are known for their good nature. When Captain James Cook visited Tonga in the 1770s, he was so well received that he dubbed them "the Friendly Islands." (Even today, it is against Tongan custom ever to ask a guest to leave a home, and the national toast *Ofatu* translates as "I love you.") Tonga plays a role in one of sailing's most infamous mutinies: it was near Ha'apai that Captain William Bligh and a group of loyal crewmen were set adrift in an open boat by mutineers led by Fletcher Christian. Bligh's party landed on the Tongan island of Kao and found the residents a bit less friendly than those Cook encountered; one of Bligh's men was killed and the others barely escaped before Bligh led them safely to Timor.

Each of Tonga's three island groups has its own personality. Tongatapu is the nation's political center, home to King Taufa'ahau Tupou IV and much of the archipelago's population. The hilly and richly wooded islands of Vava'u enjoy the majority of Tonga's tourist trade (though tourism is still a relatively undeveloped component of the economy); they provide excellent cruising grounds, and one of the best-protected harbors—Port of Refuge—in Polynesia. In the deeper water of the Vava'u islands, there's an added attraction—thousands of Antarctic humpback whales gather here from July to November to calve, giving visitors a chance to frolic among these great cetaceans. Ha'apai is less populated and developed than the other island groups. "Ha'apai is the cultural center of the Tongan people," Carl said, "the traditional homeland, with low, sandy islands and an active volcano. There are many reefs here and navigation is a bit trickier. However, it's the best place to sail a boat very fast. And that's what brought Mark and me to Ha'apai."

The craft that drew Carl to Tonga is a modern rendition of a Kalia, the traditional Tongan outrigger canoe that was once used to conquer Polynesia. Designed in the style of a proa, Kalia have two hulls, with a mast and keel on the larger of the hulls on the leeward side. It's a design built for speed and traversing reefs. There's one idiosyncrasy to sailing Kalias (and proas in general): to change course, you must "shunt" rather than tack in the traditional manner, as the outrigger portion of the boat must be kept windward.

"The Kalia is quite enmeshed in the Tongan culture," Carl continued. "Nobility would take their names from parts of the boat." With the introduction of engine-driven vessels by Europeans, Kalias were abandoned by native Tongans. However, as the year 2000 approached, the king saw an opportunity to put his tiny nation on the international scene:

as Tonga is situated near the International Date Line, it would be one of the first republics to usher in the millennium. Why not construct a traditional Tongan craft and sail it across the date line as the clock hit midnight so Tongans would be the first people to enter the year 2000? Thus, the National Kalia Project and the *Millennium* was born. The boat—106 feet in length, with a 24-by-60 foot deck—was constructed under the guidance of a native Tongan master carver named Tui'one Pulotu. (Two smaller boats, 40 feet in length, were also built.) The boat was beautifully crafted and completed in time to sail into the new century—but as a classical proa, its engineering was somewhat lacking. That's where Mark Belvedere and Carl Hosticka entered the picture. Mark was commissioned by the National Kalia Project to retrofit the *Millennium* in accordance with classical Kalia design; Carl volunteered to help establish a nonprofit to raise and administer the funds necessary for a maritime center that would honor and preserve Tonga's seafaring culture. The project is under way, and the *Millennium* will be at its center; it's hoped that the retooled Kalia will one day be used to give visitors a firsthand taste of historic Tongan life.

Helping to give Tongans a sense of their seafaring legacy has been one of Carl and Mark's passions in recent years. Another has been speed—more specifically, a desire to crack the 50-knot barrier. "Thanks to their hull design, proa have great potential as fast boats," Carl said. "The force of the wind literally lifts the boats out of the water, hence the term you'll sometimes hear, 'flying proa.' Mark wanted to see if it might be possible to build a proa that could set a world speed record on the 500-meter course. The craft utilizes a classical proa hull design and a windsurfing-style sail. We've had one sanctioned speed trial so far, but the winds were disappointingly light. It's our hope to mount another attempt in the coming year."

"One day Mark and I were out testing the proa off Ha'apai," Carl recounted, "when one of the smaller boats built by the Kalia Foundation came up alongside of us. It was crewed by a group of local men who were smiling exuberantly and singing in Tongan. As they came alongside of us, I was almost swept away with emotion. Here, speeding along on our hybridized proa, we were given the opportunity to experience a taste of a seafaring tradition many thousands of years old.

"It almost brought me to tears."

DESTINATION

42

Carl Hosticka serves as deputy council president for the Metro Council, the directly elected regional government that serves more than 1.3 million residents in twenty-five cities in the Portland, Oregon, metropolitan area. He is also a professor of public policy at the University of Oregon in Eugene. Previously, Carl worked as a lecturer in law at the State University of New York and in the Peace Corps in Nepal and India. An avid sailor, he holds a Coast Guard license to operate vessels up to a hundred tons. Carl has raced sucessfully in small boats (two-time national champion in Santana 20s) and offshore (class winner in the Swiftsure International Yacht Race). He is the founder of the Kalia Foundation USA (www.kaliafoundation.org), which was organized to raise funds for the restoration of the Millennium Kalia and to establish the Tongan Seafaring Center.

► IF YOU GO ◄

► **Getting There:** Several international airlines serve Tonga from Los Angeles, reaching the island of Tongatapu in the south via Fiji (Air Pacific) or Samoa (Air New Zealand). From Tongatapu, you'll need to fly to Vava'u via Peau Vava'u or Airlines Tonga to pick up your charter.

► **Best Time to Visit:** Tonga's tropical climate sees a bit more humidity and rain between November and April, and a bit more wind from May through October.

► **Charter Operators:** Several companies offer bareboat and skippered charters in Tonga from the island of Vava'u, including The Moorings (888-952-8420; www.moorings.com), Footloose Charter (+676 70646), and Sailing Safaris Marine Center (+676 70650).

► **Moorings:** On Vava'u, moorings can be found at The Moorings (+676 70016) and Sailing Safaris Marine Center (+676 70650).

► **On-Shore Accommodations:** Ha'apai does not have as many lodgings options as the more popular Vava'u group of islands, but a number of modest options are listed on the Tonga Visitor's Bureau Web site (www.tongaholiday.com).

THE BLUE COAST

RECOMMENDED BY **Susan Maffei Plowden**

✴

No movie has had a more negative effect on a nation's tourism efforts than the 1978 film *Midnight Express* had on Turkey—specifically, on Americans visiting Turkey. If you haven't seen the movie, good; if you have, forget about it. Because among many Mediterranean aficionados, Turkey is every bit as beautiful as Greece, with even more ruins, friendly people, and a well-organized sailing infrastructure.

"Everywhere you turn, there are great historical relics," Susan Maffei Plowden recalled of her 1992 voyage to Turkey. "The water along the Mediterranean is a series of turquoises, greens, and blues. When you find a deserted beach, you're often not alone—there's also a thousand-year-old sarcophagus half-submerged off the beach!"

Turkey, perhaps more than any nation in the world, truly straddles the borders of East and West. It's the clash and assimilation of very different cultures that makes Turkey such a fascinating tourist destination—that, and its astonishingly beautiful and unspoiled southern coast. Turkey has over 2,600 miles of coastline along its southern reaches, with the eastern third of the coast bordering on the Mediterranean, and the western two-thirds bordering on the Aegean. The stretch of the Mediterranean from Bodrum (in the west) to Antalya (in the east) is the most popular cruising route; the region along this route has been dubbed the Blue (or Turquoise) Coast. Since the prevailing winds—the meltemi—blow from north to south, most sailors choose to sail from Bodrum to Antalya. On Susan's trip, the route was reversed, though the reverse order did nothing to dampen the joy of the experience.

"We were on the very fast 135-foot J-Class sloop *Endeavour*," Susan explained, "and we made it across the Mediterranean from Crete to Antalya in just thirty-six hours. The minarets poking up from the walled port city confirmed that we were in a special place.

DESTINATION

43

Hearing the muezzin calling the faithful to prayer was a more exotic welcome than you might find in the Caribbean, where you'd likely hear a rooster crowing." Antalya dates back to the second century B.C., and was inhabited in turn by Romans, Byzantines, and Seljuks before the Ottomans took control. The 10,000-foot Bey Mountains serve as a stunning backdrop for what's become a favorite holiday destination, and many of Antalya's landmarks have been lovingly preserved, including the Yivli Minareli Mosque (c. 1300); its fluted minaret has become synonymous with the city. "Going ashore in Antalya, we were transported into another culture," Susan said. "As we walked along the cobblestone streets that wind around the city walls, rug merchants offered us cups of cay, the traditional Turkish apple tea. It's polite to accept, and after some conversation—the shopkeepers speak fairly good English—you're expected to look at their rugs. A normal person may return to the boat with one rug. Our friend went back with a dozen. Experiencing the culture of bargaining was fun."

Leaving Antalya, the Blue Coast dips to the southwest. "There were many islands to tuck in behind as we hugged the coast," Susan continued, "and many gullets—the traditional Turkish boat, snub-nosed like a Baltic Trader—motor-sailing along. Our next stop was Phaselis, which was a thriving port in the seventh century B.C. The ruins there—a theater, a row of stores, an aqueduct, among others—were virtually untouched. This was where we came upon the marble sarcophagi in the water by the beach, again unblemished. I couldn't help thinking at the time that in the U.S., such treasures wouldn't exist. They'd either be taken or tagged with graffiti. The three natural harbors there were surrounded by pine forests, more like Maine than the Mediterranean."

One of the high points of Susan's Blue Coast adventure came after arriving in the town of Ekincik. "We met an old friend whose husband owns the Sardes Tourism fleet that runs visitors up the Dalyan River to take in the ruins at Caunos. We anchored *Endeavour* at the mouth of the river, and then a motorboat zipped us up the river. We came around a corner, and suddenly there was one of the most amazing sights I'd ever seen—intricate tombs carved high into the cliffs." According to Turkish tourist guide Burak Sansal, the tombs are "sculpted in the form of the porticoes of small Ionic temples, among the most splendid examples of Lycian-type funerary architecture in Turkey." The tombs' original occupants are believed to have been of Carian descent, though archeological evidence suggests that the tombs were used later for the Roman dead.

OPPOSITE
For sailors,
Turkey offers
incredible history
and beauty—
and none of
the horrors
depicted
in Midnight
Express.

DESTINATION

43

No trip to Turkey is complete without a Turkish bath, and in Marmaris, the guests on *Endeavour* got their chance. "Walking through a maze of back alleys and covered bazaars, we came across a sign—'Be a Sultan for One Day.' For seven dollars, they sponge you off and beat you with reeds. It was 90 degrees and 90 percent humidity. Who could resist?"

Susan Maffei Plowden grew up sailing on Long Island Sound before moving to Nantucket, where she learned the fine art of painting and varnishing wooden boats. From there she spent a number of years delivering yachts to the Caribbean and Mediterranean, as well as working on sailing-school ships, before coming ashore in Jamestown, Rhode Island. Now she is a media/PR, marketing, and sponsorship consultant with a focus on international yachting events and clients. Susan has worked on a number of America's Cup campaigns, Whitbread/Volvo Ocean Races, and other Grand Prix events that have enabled her to spend time sailing in some of the more spectacular parts of the world. But for total relaxation she and her husband, John, sail *Grace*, their 1926 Herreshoff 12-1/2, on Narragansett Bay.

> **IF YOU GO**

➤ **Getting There:** Most cruisers will begin their adventures in Bodrum. Bodrum is served by Turkish Airlines, with connections from Istanbul, which is served by many major carriers, including American Airlines, British Airways, and Lufthansa.

➤ **Best Time to Visit:** The Blue Coast of Turkey has a Mediterranean climate, with the promise of sun from April to October. July and particularly August can be quite warm if you go ashore.

➤ **Charter Operators:** Turkey has many bareboat charter options along the coast. In Bodrum, these include Pupa Yachting (+90 252 316 7715; www.pupa.com.tr).

➤ **Moorings:** Moorings available in Bodrum include Bodrum Milta Karada Marina (+90 252 316 1860/66, www.miltabodrummarina.com).

➤ **On-Shore Accommodations:** The Turkish Department of Culture and Tourism (212-687-2194; www.tourismturkey.org) provides an overview of lodgings options throughout the country.

BRITISH VIRGIN ISLANDS

RECOMMENDED BY **Tanya Whistler**

Easy. Comfortable. Beautiful. A few reasons why the British Virgin Islands are home to the world's largest yacht charter fleet . . . and are one of the world's most sought-after cruising destinations.

"The British Virgin Islands promote themselves as 'the Sailing Capital of the World,'" Tanya Whistler said, "and the numbers seem to support that claim. Digging deeper, beyond marketing slogans, I think there are a number of reasons that the BVI are so appealing to so many cruisers. First, the experience the region offers is very accessible to entry-level sailors. The anchorages are very easy, the distances between anchorages are short, and the seas are low. Second, the BVI are convenient. They're close to the United States, the U.S. dollar can be used here, people speak English. French Martinique, for example, is a bit outside of some people's comfort zone. On Tortola, you can pick up CNN. Finally, there's a broad range of experiences to be had here. Once people have cruised here a few times and built up their confidence, they can come and explore the more secluded coasts and find new reasons to come back. And if other parties in the group are a little less keen on sailing, they can go diving, bonefishing, marlin fishing, kiteboarding—the possibilities are almost limitless."

The Virgin Islands take their name from Christopher Columbus, who for reasons unknown was thinking of Saint Ursula when he came upon them in 1493 (the legend of Saint Ursula goes that she had a following of 11,000 virgin maids). There are roughly fifty (not 11,000) islands in the British Virgin Island chain, which rests sixty miles east of Puerto Rico, on the cusp between the Atlantic to the north and the Caribbean to the south. The largest islands of the BVI are Tortola, Virgin Gorda, Anegada, and Jost Van Dyke.

DESTINATION

44

Great Britain acquired (some might say wrested) the BVI from the Dutch in 1672, and they remain to this day an overseas territory of the U.K. Before the Brits and the Dutch possessed them, Spain, France, and Denmark all laid various claims to the islands, which were valued at first as a foothold in the New World, and later for their potential to raise sugar cane. Though sugar cane was rendered largely irrelevant with the widespread cultivation of the sugar beet in the United States and Europe in the early 1800s, the residents of the BVI continued to sustain themselves with agriculture for the next century and a half. In the last forty years, tourism and financial services—the latter abetted by rather flexible tax and governance laws under the International Business Companies Act—have displaced agriculture. Tourism accounts for roughly 45 percent of the economy.

Many charter operations are based on Tortola, the largest of the BVI, and this island is a likely point of departure for bareboaters—though you may wish to delay departure a bit to take in some of the island's fine beaches. Upon departure, sailors will find healthy (but manageable) winds blowing to the southeast, and a pleasing variety of venues in a comfortingly finite 32-by-15-mile cruising area. Tanya places the cruisers that leave Tortola's docks into two very general categories: the party people, and the honeymoon or already-have-kids people. "The party people tend to spend a lot of time on Jost Van Dyke," Tanya continued. "There are lots of lively nightspots there." This island takes its name from a former Dutch pirate, which may speak to its devil-may-care ambiance. Favorite watering holes include the Soggy Dollar Bar, which is said to have created the Painkiller, a rum concoction that's one of the BVI's most enduring contributions to bartending annals. Gertrude's and Foxy's are two other celebrated bars. Jost Van Dyke has three protected, easy anchorages that facilitate shore landings and leavings for the slightly befuddled: Great Harbor is home to Foxy's, White Bay home to the Soggy Dollar and Gertrude's. (Jost Van Dyke has plentiful white sand beaches for sleeping off the previous night's revelry—or for spending the night, for that matter.)

While on the subject of bars and the BVI, one cannot forego mention of the *William Thornton*—or the *Willie T*, as it's affectionately known. The *Willie T* is a floating bar and eatery perpetually anchored in the Bight at Norman Island. It takes its name from a one-time resident of Jost Van Dyke who made his way to the then brand-new United States and designed the United States capitol building. The original *Willie T*, an aging Baltic Trader, was launched in 1989 in its new incarnation, and was a fast success. It eventually sprang a leak and slowly sank, to be replaced with a 100-foot schooner with substantially

OPPOSITE
The British Virgin Islands offer tremendous cruising diversity in a compact space—one reason they're the most popular charter destination in the world.

DESTINATION

44

more room . . . and a steel hull. There's a large aft bridge deck, and many *Willie T* visitors experience such exuberance at the prospect of whiling away an afternoon at this floating pub that they feel compelled to leap off. If the visitor is female and willing to take the plunge *au naturel*, she will be rewarded with a complimentary *William Thornton* T-shirt.

For those who are seeking a slightly less rambunctious adventure, the BVI offer count-less quiet bays where one can tuck in without the slightest fear of having an overzealous barkeep pour a "body shot" of vodka anywhere upon your person. "Diamond Key is quite secluded," Tanya continued, "with just one restaurant ashore. Generally, there are only a handful of boats there. Anegada is another quiet spot. Where many BVI islands are quite hilly, Anegada is completely flat. It's circled by a large coral reef that requires a bit of preparation to pass through, but once you're inside, you'll get a taste of the old-time Caribbean. Which is to say, aside from a few little restaurants on the beach that serve grilled lobster, there's nothing happening." Anegada has been set aside as a wildlife sanc-tuary, providing habitat for roseate flamingoes, herons, and ospreys. It's also the sole ter-rain of the Anegada rock iguana, an endangered reptile that can grow to six feet (they're harmless).

The list of "must-see" BVI attractions goes on and on. On Virgin Gorda there are the Baths, a formation of granite boulders that have created a number of secluded grottoes and pools where one can snorkel about; on Norman Island there are the Caves, another celebrated snorkeling site believed to have provided inspiration for Robert Louis Steven-son's *Treasure Island*. Scuba-diving sailors will certainly want to make a trip to the Wreck of the *Rhone* near Peter Island, a Royal Mail Steamer that sank in 1867 but is still mostly intact and quite visible.

Many people come to the BVI for a working vacation of sorts—that is, to learn to sail. A number of schools allow students to gain essential skills while they enjoy the north Caribbean's many bounties. Should these newbies gain sufficient skills, they may wish to participate in one of the BVI's few racing events, the BVI Spring Regatta and Sailing Festival. The event seems to be in keeping with the easygoing atmosphere of the BVI; the event's organizers promise "six days of nonstop racing action and seven nights of partying."

Tanya Whistler started working with SunSail in 1991 as a receptionist, thinking she would have a leisurely summer "messing around on boats." Fifteen years later she's still with the company! After holding various roles within the company, she now serves as the director of SunSail's Tortola operations. "Most of my energies have been focused on uniting the Moorings and Sunsail brands under the First Choice banner," Tanya said. "I am lucky enough to be based in Tortola, and get to work closely with customers, local staff, and our offices around the world."

IF YOU GO

➤ **Getting There:** Most bareboat charters begin on the island of Tortola. To reach Tortola, U.S. residents must connect from Puerto Rico, St. Thomas, or St. Martin. Service is provided by many major carriers, including American, Continental, Delta, and United Airlines.

➤ **Best Time to Visit:** The BVI have a subtropical climate, with sunshine and warm temperatures throughout the year. Winds are a bit stronger in the winter months, when many seek a retreat from the cold. Severe storms are always a possibility in the fall.

➤ **Charter Operators:** The BVI are the most popular charter destination in the world, and offer multitudinous charter options. In addition to Tanya's employer, SunSail (888-350-3568; www.sunsail.com), see the list provided at www.bvitourism.com/charters/bareboat.

➤ **Moorings:** The islands of the BVI have countless mooring options. A very comprehensive list is provided on the BVI Tourist Board Web site, www.bvitourism.com/moorings.

➤ **On-Shore Accommodations:** The BVI Tourist Board (800-835-8530; www.bvitourism.com/accommodations) has extensive lists of accommodations on the various islands.

DESTINATION

44

THE SOLENT AND BEYOND

RECOMMENDED BY **Adrian Morgan**

✴

Though remnants of sailing craft have been found in Egypt dating back to 2600 B.C. (and perhaps even earlier), most place the birth of recreational sailing some four thouand years later, during the reign of Charles II. After being coaxed to return to Britain from his exile in Holland to take up the throne after Cromwell's overthrow of his father some eleven years before, Charles II sought to make a glamorous entry—and he chose a sleek Dutch *Jachtschip* for his debut. By all accounts, his coming out was a great success, and Charles II went on to champion the notion of sailing for pleasure. The sport continued to be favored by English monarchs, gaining a more popular following during the reigns of King George IV and Queen Victoria, when a fleet of ships was maintained at the royal residence on the Isle of Wight, bordering a stretch of the English Channel between the island and the mainland called the Solent . . . a region that's widely considered to be the cradle of yachting.

"As the Alps are to skiing, so is the Solent to sailing," commented Adrian Morgan. "You'll see many boats in the Solent, and anchorages can be full at peak times. But off peak the Solent can be remarkably empty, and you have this feeling of sailing where heroes have gone before. Nelson departed for Trafalgar from Southsea; the *Mary Rose* sank off Portsmouth. Invasion fleets headed for French beaches from the Beaulieu River and other places that in peacetime were the haunt of gulls and wooden yachts. To sail here, in short, is to share yachting's history. Every day, you see the great yachts of the day tuning up. It's where a group of Americans took on a fleet of the best British yachts and beat them, and where round-the-world races start and finish. It's the test bed of ideas; a place to see first-hand all that's new and exciting in this sport. Beyond that, the Solent is a truly challenging piece of water to race and sail on. To paraphrase Dr. Johnson's remark about London: When you're tired of the Solent you're tired of sailing."

OPPOSITE

Festivities under full sail off the Isle of Wight during Cowes Race Week.

DESTINATION

45

The Solent stretches along the mainland from Lymington in the west to just beyond Portsmouth Harbour in the east. Millennia ago, the Solent was a river valley, formed by the River Frome. Written records from Caesar's time intimate that it was once possible to wade across the Solent from the mainland to the Isle of Wight during low tide. Alluvial flow and the slow sinking of southeast England have widened and deepened the channel; even at its most narrow point, its width is nearly a mile. Though the Solent is buffered from the English Channel by the Isle of Wight, the swirling currents created by complex tidal patterns and the inflow of several rivers—and the presence of Bramble Bank near the center of the passage—make for tricky navigation. The city of Portsmouth, thanks to its strategic location vis-à-vis France and its narrow harbor entrance (which enabled easy fortification), has long been the home of the Royal Navy.

While Portsmouth is rich in nautical lore and Southampton is a major port, the Solent's sailing capital is unquestionably the Isle of Wight town of Cowes. It was here that the Royal Yacht Club (later known as the Royal Yacht Squadron) was established in 1815, and with it the world's longest-running regatta, now known as Cowes Race Week; while the first official regatta was held here in 1812, the three-day regatta held in 1826 is considered the formal beginning of Race Week. It was also here that the first America's Cup race was conducted. Today, more than a thousand yachts take part in seven days of racing during Cowes Race Week, competing in over fifty classes during early August. Events are presided over by the RYS from its clubhouse, the Squadron Castle. Some races are started by blasts from the castle's William IV cannon, which once rested on the *HMS Royal Adelaide*.

The Solent and Cowes rest at the front and center of yachting history. But they're not the only sailing attraction in the south of England. "The Dorset Coast is perhaps the most beautiful in the south," Adrian opined. "It's rugged and forbidding, with few refuges, but it is amongst my favorites." The coast of Dorset is marked by its curious land forms, which chronicle nearly 200 million years of geologic developments. (This historic significance has earned the region the nickname "Jurassic Coast," and UNESCO World Heritage Site status.) The land's fascinating formations include Lulworth Cove, a picture-perfect example of a natural cove, almost exactly concentric with a small opening to the sea, and Durdle Door, a natural arch that would seem more at home in southern Utah than along the English coast. Both are near the town of West Lulworth.

Continuing west along the coast beyond Dorset, one reaches the county of Cornwall and the West Country. "The West Country is magic for its rivers, its pubs by the waterside, its soft air, and its sense of timelessness," Adrian went on. "And for that matter, its history. Drake fought the Spanish Armada off these shores, and chased them to Dover and beyond—after finishing his game of bowls. It was once the haunt of pirates and wreckers; it's no coincidence that Daphne du Maurier set her novel *Rebecca* here."

The West Country's nautical center is the town of Falmouth, which boasts one of the world's largest natural harbors (when combined with the waters of Carrick Roads). "It's fed by a number of rivers—including the Fal—and the town itself is lively and steeped in history," Adrian continued. "There's still a fleet of old oyster dredgers working the harbor; they dredge under sail. Each year, there's a festival of traditional boats in August. Much of the sailing is on the rivers that feed the harbor; it seems that whatever estuary or river you enter, there's a pub not far away with a mooring." Falmouth is also home to the National Maritime Museum. Its collection of more than two million seafaring and navigation objects makes it one of the world's most prominent nautical museums.

Adrian recounted one memory that speaks to the quiet sailing pleasures of the West Country and England's south coast. "It was near Falmouth—to the east, in the same harbor," Adrian recalled. "I found myself in a little offshoot of the harbor near the town of St. Mawes called the Percuil River with my boat—the *Sally*—and another old wooden boat, the *Sabrina*, owned by a friend. It was early evening, approaching dusk. Together we slowly sailed up the river, two quintessential cruising boats from the 1930s. There was hardly any wind, and nary a word passed between us. Eventually we grounded gently on the mud. We silently sipped a toast, then adjourned to a nearby pub.

"I suppose we were racing, though neither of us would've admitted it."

Adrian Morgan spent twenty-five years working in London on magazines and newspapers, covering sailing and writing travel stories. He was yachting correspondent for the *Daily Mail* and the *European*, and now writes a monthly column for *Classic Boat*. For ten years he has owned a seventy-year-old wooden boat that was based on the South Coast until a job opportunity on the *Scotsman* newspaper took him (and *Sally*) north. After Edinburgh he ventured even further north and spent a year learning to build wooden boats; he now builds his own wooden boats to a Norwegian design on a farm near Ullapool. While running Viking Boats of Ullapool (www.viking-boats.com), he still writes about sailing from a croft house in the Highlands, which he shares with his partner, Rona, and his short-haired pointer, Bran.

IF YOU GO

➤ **Getting There:** The Solent borders the southern coast along Southampton and Portsmouth. It's roughly two hours by car or train from London, which is served by most major carriers. There are hundreds of ferry crossings each day to the Isle of Wight.

➤ **Best Time to Visit:** Conditions are most conducive to sailing from mid-spring through mid-fall. Cowes and the Solent see their greatest excitement in early August of each year, when Skandia Cowes Race Week occurs.

➤ **Charter Operators:** There are many options for charters around the Solent. SunSail (888-350-3568; www.sunsail.com) operates from Port Solent; Firstaway Specialist Yacht Charters (+44 23 8023 6000; www.firstaway.co.uk) is in Southhampton.

➤ **Moorings:** There are ample facilities throughout this section of the world, both on the mainland and on the Isle of Wight. For the latter, berths are available at Cowes Yacht Haven (+44 1983 299975; www.cowesyachthaven.com) and Folly Reach Pontoons (+44 788 772 5922), among other marinas.

➤ **On-Shore Accommodations:** A comprehensive list of accommodations on the island can be found at Isle of Wight Tourism (+44 1983 813800; www.islandbreaks.co.uk).

DESTINATION

45

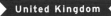
SOUTH GEORGIA ISLAND

RECOMMENDED BY **Skip Novak**

Mountaineering and open-ocean racing are not areas of expertise that are mutually exclusive, though the subset of adventurers who have mastered both skills is rather finite. For this elite group—which includes Skip Novak—a place like South Georgia Island holds special appeal.

"I visited South Georgia for the first time in 1988," Skip recounted. "I had built a sturdy boat—the *Pelagic*—with some partners. The boat was mine to use the first year, and I chose to take it to Tierra del Fuego, then Antarctica, then South Georgia, and then Cape Town. My goal in visiting South Georgia was to conduct some mountaineering expeditions. I was very influenced by the life of Bill Tilman, a great seafarer and mountaineer. I had been climbing in New Zealand and the Alps, and was interested in remote mountain areas. South Georgia has many such areas, and of course it can only be accessed by boat."

South Georgia is one of the most isolated islands in the world. It rests nearly 1,300 miles east of Tierra del Fuego, and some 800 miles east of the Falkland Islands, on the same latitudinal line as Cape Horn. "From a sailing perspective, it represents a tremendous commitment to get to South Georgia," Skip continued. "Even compared to the Antarctic Peninsula, it's much more isolated. Once you've set off, you've burned your bridges for going back. The sailing can be very tough, as the katabatic winds are prevailing. Depressions curve to the north as they head east, bringing in big low-pressure systems and, in turn, rough weather. It's a rough sailing trip—a long five or six days—especially on the way back." The island is long and narrow, roughly 100 miles long and alternating from just one mile to 25 miles in width. Several mountain ranges extend along its center, such as Allardyce and Salvesen, which include eleven peaks higher than

6,500 feet. During the island's brief summer, most of the ground remains cloaked in glaciers, ice caps, and snowfields.

The first European to view South Georgia was a London merchant named Antoine de la Roche, who took shelter near the island in 1675 after losing his way around Cape Horn. One hundred years later, Captain Cook came upon the island, thinking he had finally identified the last great continent. He was, of course, mistaken, and he named the island for King George. Cook's reports of great numbers of whales and seals in the waters around South Georgia brought first sealers and then whalers. The whaling onslaught began in earnest in the early 1900s. The world's greatest concentration of whales—blue, fin, sei, humpback, and southern right—were reduced to a mere 10 percent (or less) of their former populations. In 1974, these species received protection under the International Whaling Convention, and their numbers are slowly increasing. Sperm whales and orcas (killer whales), less impacted by industrialized whaling, are also seen in the waters off South Georgia. At the heyday of the whaling boom, two thousand people called South Georgia home; now it is uninhabited.

South Georgia is a birder's paradise. Eighty-one different species have been documented, including albatrosses, cape and giant petrels, Antarctic prions, and many, many, many macaroni, gentoo, and king penguins. Scientists place the island's seabird population at more than thirty million! There's little land-mammal life on South Georgia beyond rats, mice, and a few herds of reindeer, all of which were introduced. Pinnipeds, however, are another matter. Though hunted to near extinction during the nineteenth century, both elephant seal and fur seal have recovered marvelously; the fur seal population is placed at over three million.

"The masses of wildlife along the shoreline of South Georgia are overwhelming," Skip added. "Albatrosses, seals, penguins. Sometimes we'll go close to shore and there will be hundreds of thousands of these animals. When we make landing for a tour, we'll combine visits to wildlife sites with trips to abandoned whaling stations. We try to spend a couple days in each place, weather permitting, as sailing up and down the coast of South Georgia is quite taxing. Twenty miles can be very difficult to cover. Most of the animal species are present in each place we anchor, so there's no great advantage to moving frequently. When you're in a place like South Georgia, you have to be extremely cautious. If something goes wrong, there's no rescue service whatsoever. You're on your own.

OPPOSITE

The mountainous terrain of South Georgia Island attracts sailors who also love climbing.

DESTINATION

46

"There has been more than one occasion when I've been trying to lead us from one anchorage to another. It's blowing like hell, and with the fog and/or snow, you can't see anything. We're cold, exhausted, utterly spent. Eventually, we get to the next anchorage. As I fall asleep, I'm wondering, 'What are we doing here?!' The next morning we wake up and have beautiful bright conditions, and the boat is surrounded by seals and penguins. I sit with a cup of coffee or tea and reflect on this place of great contrasts."

Since he began leading charter trips in the region, Skip Novak has led many climbers and trekkers to South Georgia. In January of 2005, he led a special expedition—the quest to scale an unclimbed mountain. "We sailed from the Falklands to South Georgia on the original *Pelagic*," Skip recalled, "and then a four-man team was dropped in Larsen Harbor. From there, we did an eighteen-day ski traverse to the bottom part of the island, with the plan to ascend some previously unclimbed peaks en route." Skip and his crew were successful, as reported in the March 2006 *South Georgia Newsletter*:

> The Antarctic Place-Names Committee has accepted Skip Novak's proposal that Peak 5680 which Julian Freeman-Attwood and his team climbed, including Skip Novak, on their British South Georgia Expedition 2005 should be called Mount Pelagic. The Commissioner for GSGSSI approved his proposal. It has been added to the SGSSI Gazetteer and is now available for official use . . . [T]he name Mount Pelagic reflects the contribution the yacht Pelagic and Skip Novak, its owner and skipper, have made over a number of years and continue to do so in terms of supporting expeditions and yacht cruises.

Skip Novak is best known for his participation in four Whitbread Round the World Yacht Races since 1977. In that year at the age of twenty-five he navigated the British Cutter *Kings Legend* to second place. Skippering the *Independent Endeavour* in 1979, he won the Parmelia Race from Plymouth to Fremantle, Australia. He skippered Simon Le Bon's *Drum* in the 1985–86 Whitbread Race, coming in third. Skip wrote *One Watch at a Time* about this experience and it was published simultaneously in England and in America. In 1989 he was project manager and skipper of the *Fazisi*, the first Soviet entry in the Whitbread Race, and he chronicled this watershed event in his book *Fazisi, The Joint Venture*, which was shortlisted for the William Hill Sports Book of the Year Award in Britain. Wishing to combine his mountaineering skills with sailing, he built the expedition yacht

Pelagic in 1987, and has since spent seventeen seasons in Antarctic waters, twelve of which involved leading combined climbing and filming projects based from the vessel. Skip has occasionally returned to top-level ocean racing, navigating the French catamaran *Explorer* to a sailing record in the 1997 Transpac Race from Los Angeles to Honolulu (5 days, 9 hours). In 1998, he coskippered *Explorer* with Bruno Peyron, breaking the sailing record from Yokohama to San Francisco (14 days, 17 hours). In January to March 2001 he coskippered the French catamaran *Innovation Explorer* to a second place in the millennium nonstop, no-limits circumnavigation, The Race. In 2002–03 Skip project-managed the construction of his new *Pelagic Australis*, a 23-meter purpose-built expedition vessel for high-latitude sailing, in order to augment the charter operations of the original *Pelagic*. Launched in September of 2003, she is the flagship for Pelagic Expeditions.

IF YOU GO

➤ **Getting There:** Sailing expeditions to South Georgia begin in the town of Stanley on the Falkland Islands, and last a minimum of 21 days. Stanley can be reached from the Chilean town of Punta Arenas via LanChile. Punta Arenas can be reached via Santiago by LanExpress and Sky Airline. Skip Novak recommends International Tours and Travel (jf.itt@horizon.co.fk) for advice and arrangements for arrival in the Falklands.

➤ **Best Time to Visit:** It's possible to make the passage to South Georgia from October to May, though high summer (November to March) will have the best weather.

➤ **Charter Operators:** Skip Novak's Pelagic Sailing Expeditions (www.pelagic.co.uk) leads 21- and 28-day expeditions to South Georgia; Expedition Sail (888-250-4862; www.expeditionsail.com) leads slightly longer trips.

➤ **Moorings:** There are no facilities on South Georgia Island.

➤ **On-Shore Accommodations:** Punta Arenas has a number of lodgings options, including the Hotel Nogueira (+56 61 248840; www.hotelnogueira.com). Stanley has several options, including the Malvina House Hotel (+500 21355; www.malvinahousehotel.com) and the Upland Goose Hotel (+500 21455).

DESTINATION

46

LAKE CHAMPLAIN

RECOMMENDED BY **Justin Assad**

For not quite three weeks in 1998, Lake Champlain was America's newest Great Lake. The designation—part of an effort to secure additional federal resources engineered by Vermont Senator Patrick Leahy—was quickly struck down, returning the lake to its original status as merely a large and exceedingly scenic lake. Many sailors, though, continue to view Champlain as great, official designation or not.

"I took the job as sailing coach for the University of Vermont in Burlington before ever sailing on Lake Champlain," said Justin Assad. "It wasn't long before I fell in love with the place. With the Adirondack Mountains to the west and the Green Mountains to the east, it's hard to imagine a more beautiful place to sail. From a racing standpoint, Champlain is an excellent training venue, as you can give sailors an incredible variety of conditions—from flat water that simulates smaller-pond sailing (something you see from time to time on the collegiate circuit), to 6-foot waves and a 20-knot breeze, the kind of weather we get when big fall storms come out of the southwest. Many college sailing venues are limited in terms of what they offer; we have a huge expanse of water to work with. The climate here in northern New England gives us a work-hard focus. We have limited time to practice, as winter can arrive by mid-November and stay through early spring. However, we're out on the water until November 18 and back out again soon after ice-out. I think this makes our team quite resilient. We've gone down to regattas in Boston in the spring when everyone is wearing dry suits, and we're just in our foul-weather gear!"

Lake Champlain is a long, narrow body of fresh water extending 110 miles from its northernmost point just inside the province of Quebec to its southern terminus near Whitehall, New York. Never more than 12 miles wide, the lake forms more than half of the border between upstate New York and Vermont, and is the sixth-largest lake in the lower forty-eight. It takes its name from the French explorer Samuel de Champlain, who came upon it in 1609, venturing south from Quebec.

Thanks to its strategic location between the St. Lawrence and Hudson Rivers, Lake Champlain played a crucial role in early American history, both in the development of commerce and in three military campaigns. During the French-Indian War—which, for all intents and purposes, was a battle between France and England for control of the New World—British General Jeffrey Amherst crossed the lake en route to his conquest of Quebec City and Montreal, victories that won Canada for the crown. Early in the Revolutionary War, the Battle of Valcour Bay was fought off Valcour Island, near current-day Plattsburgh, New York, in what many consider to be the nascent American navy's first real engagement. (The British hoped to gain control of Lake Champlain so they could connect forces in Canada with those in New York City, which was under their control in 1776.) While little was left of America's slapdash fleet once the battle concluded, British forces were sufficiently delayed by the colonialists' inexperienced sailors to postpone their push south until the following spring. By that time, American forces had regrouped and were able to rebuff the redcoats at Saratoga. During the War of 1812, American forces again engaged the British navy near Plattsburgh, in what became known as the Battle of Lake Champlain. U.S. Navy Commodore Thomas Macdonough dealt the British a bitter defeat in September of 1814, resulting in America gaining definitive control of the lake, and a better bargaining position in treaty negotiations.

Lake Champlain's cold depths—and its rich maritime history—have created a unique museum, one that requires visitors to don scuba gear and dive down to the exhibits. A number of nineteenth-century craft that met an untimely end (or simply wore out) have been wonderfully preserved in their sunken state, and the Lake Champlain Underwater Historic Preserve provides access to the wrecks. Maps and moorings are provided, and divers are encouraged to visit (but never touch or swim inside) the boats, which include the *O.J. Walker*, a schooner-rigged canal sailboat designed for carrying freight across the lake and into the canal connecting Lake Champlain to the Hudson (built in 1862, sunk in 1895); the *Water Witch*, initially built as a steamboat and later converted into a schooner (built in 1832, sunk in 1866); and the *Spitfire*, a gondola gunboat that was sunk by the British in the aforementioned Battle of Valcour in 1776. The mast of the *Spitfire* still stands, and its bow gun stands ready to ward off any ghostly redcoats that remain;

209

it has been designated an "American Treasure" by the National Trust for Historic Preservation.

The lakeshore adjoining Burlington, Vermont, an eccentric college town that was the original home of Ben & Jerry's ice cream and of colorful Socialist mayor (now Congressman) Bernie Sanders, is overflowing with New England charm. "We can't always take advantage of our surroundings," Justin continued, "but on occasion we're able to combine work with play. On one occasion two falls ago we were able to push down to Shelburne Bay, about fifteen miles south, during practice. It was hard going, but wonderful to see a different spot. Sometimes we can turn practice into a run up to Appletree Bay to the north of Burlington. As you might imagine, in the fall the colors are amazing." In addition to Shelburne and Appletree Bay, Mallet's Bay (also north) is a hotbed of sailing activity. "They have some of the best Lightning sailors in the country racing out of Mallet's Bay," Justin added.

Most of us who've stood in line at the supermarket have read in leading periodicals like the *Enquirer* of a few of the exploits of the Loch Ness Monster. Should you make it to Lake Champlain, take heed, lest you encounter Champ, the lake's own monster, replete with fuzzy photographs, occasional tabloid television coverage, and rampant rumors. Port Henry, on the New York side of the lake, is said to be a favorite swimming ground of Champ, who some cryptozoologists have speculated is a plesiosaur; others think the alleged creature could be a giant sturgeon (even Samuel de Champlain reported a sighting of such a creature nearly four hundred years ago).

While he's yet to come upon Champ (the unofficial mascot of the University of Vermont Sailing Team), Justin has witnessed sailors' encounters with other monsters from Lake Champlain's depths. "We have a species of fish that has invaded the lake from the St. Lawrence River called lamprey," Justin explained. "They're not pleasant creatures; they have an eel-like body and no head to speak of, and they attach themselves to fish and suck their blood out. Sometimes when we're out toward the middle of the lake where the water is coldest, lampreys will come up and attach themselves to a boat. When we have freshman sailors out there, or sailors from another college, it's almost inevitable that at some point in the afternoon I'll hear a high-pitched shriek.

"To date, it's always been a lamprey, not Champ."

Justin Assad began coaching the University of Vermont Sailing Team during the fall of 2003, after graduating from Columbia University that spring. He was captain of Columbia's sailing team during a resurgence that saw Columbia Sailing's first Ivy League championship and their emergence as a competitive collegiate program. He has spent five summers coaching at the East Greenwich Yacht Club in Rhode Island, working with both the Opti and 420 teams. Justin is currently a regional and assistant national team coach for the United States Optimist Dinghy Association, and has experience coaching many major Opti and 420 regattas. He is active in the Vanguard 15 class and at United States Team Racing Association events.

IF YOU GO

➤ **Getting There:** Burlington, Vermont, is a pleasant college town on the eastern shore of Lake Champlain, and is served by many major carriers, including Continental, Delta, Northwest, and United Airlines.

➤ **Best Time to Visit:** While Justin and the University of Vermont Sailing Team are on the water through mid-November, most would find conditions most pleasing from mid-May to mid-October.

➤ **Charter Operators:** Winds of Ireland (800-458-9301; www.windsofireland.net) has bareboat rentals and chartered sailing from the center of Burlington. The Lake Champlain Community Sailing Center (802-864-2499; www.communitysailingcenter.org) has small boats for hourly rental.

➤ **Moorings:** Champlain Marina (800-240-4034; www.champlainmarina.com) north of Burlington in Colchester has berths with full services for traveling sailors. The Lake Champlain Community Sailing Center (802-864-2499; www.communitysailingcenter.org) and the Burlington Community Boathouse (802-865-3377) in downtown Burlington have dock space with limited services.

➤ **On-Shore Accommodations:** The Lake Champlain Regional Chamber of Commerce (877-686-5253; www.vermont.org) lists many lodgings options in Burlington and along Lake Champlain's Vermont shore.

DESTINATION

47

NHA TRANG

RECOMMENDED BY **Kevin Quilty**

For moviegoers, the idea of cruising in Vietnam may conjure up images from *Apocalypse Now* of U.S. soldiers (played by Martin Sheen and Laurence Fishburne) motoring up a jungle river, anticipating fire from Viet Cong snipers and ultimately finding despair and death.

Things have changed.

In 2006, a 60-mile stretch of coastline adjoining the Khánh Hòa province was opened for yachts to cruise unescorted—a first for the area since the war. "I'd heard great stories from people who'd traveled to Nha Trang, Khánh Hòa's major city," said Kevin Quilty, who manages Southeast Asian operations for SunSail from Phuket. "I visited and toured the region with a speedboat. There were many off-lying islands, deep bays, and very clear, clean water—in short, phenomenal cruising grounds. We saw a fantastic opportunity to connect sailors with a desirable part of the world that had previously been off limits. Nha Trang seemed a perfect base for operations thanks to the superb sailing conditions, beautiful beaches, and famous off-lying islands like Hon Tre, Hon Yen, and Hon Rua. Unlike many places in Asia, there's a very steady and reliable wind here, which is ideal for cruisers."

Khánh Hòa is situated in south central Vietnam; the cruising area is marked by Cam Ranh Bay to the south and Van Thang Bay to the north, with Nha Trang geographically (and logistically) in the center. More than fifty islands of varying sizes adorn the coastline, which has been likened by some to parts of Hawaii—Hawaii dotted with occasional French colonial mansions! Though some high-end resorts have been developed on the mainland coast and on a few islands, they are more the exception than the rule. "You're more likely to find small restaurants serving local seafood and modest resorts than five-star

DESTINATION

48

properties," Kevin added. Nha Trang was a strategic base for U.S. forces during the Vietnam War (or what the Vietnamese people call the American War). "Though physical remnants of the war are few," Kevin said, "it's very interesting to visit places that played a role in the conflict. For many of us of a certain age, it's one of the most significant facets of history that we lived through and know."

Sailing visitors to the Khánh Hòa region will begin by provisioning themselves in the markets of Nha Trang, where one is likely to encounter some novel foodstuffs. One such rarity is Thanh Long (Green Dragon fruit), which is grown in orchards in the region. (Visitors are strongly advised to provision in Nha Trang, as there are few other options going north or south.) While in Nha Trang, you may choose to pay a visit to the temple of Po Nagar, a goddess of local origin said to have created earth, eaglewood, and rice. Parts of the temple date back to around 800 A.D. (The temple, initially built by Hindus who inhabited this area during the Champa reign, is used by local Buddhists today.) You needn't sail far to sample some of the great beauty that's destined to make Vietnam a treasured cruising ground for years to come. Nha Trang Bay is considered one of Asia's most breathtaking bays; even the beach in the center of town draws visitors from many parts of east Asia. The powdery white sand of Doc Let Beach on the Hon Khoi peninsula north of Nha Trang is a slice of paradise. There are several small resorts here. A bit farther north, you'll reach Hon Ong, which boasts a French-run resort that serves as an excellent base for exploring the nearby islands.

Several islands along the Khánh Hòa coast—including Hon Dung, Hon Cau, and Hon Yen—are home to vast numbers of *salangane*, or swifts. The nests of the swifts are considered to have healing (and even aphrodisiac) properties and thus are esteemed as great delicacies. They have little taste unto themselves, and are generally served in soups or other dishes. Swifts' nests are not fashioned from twigs and mud, as one might expect, but from the birds' saliva. They come in two varieties, white and red. The red variety is especially valuable (the source of the red is the blood that the birds cough up in an effort to create enough saliva to fashion a nest). Nest collectors scale hillsides that might reach hundreds of feet in height on shaky bamboo ladders—it's a rather hazardous occupation, and each year collectors fall to their death. The occupation is generally passed down from father to son. The nests from Vietnam are exported to the markets of Hong Kong or Taiwan, where top-quality nests can bring nearly $1,000 a pound. (It's believed that a group of power brokers in Hong Kong control the international trade in birds' nests.)

One of the most striking aspects of sailing in Vietnam is that visitors are truly engaging in a groundbreaking experience. "Almost all the anchorages you'll find are deserted," Kevin explained. "There are simply no other yachts or pleasure boats out there; you're on your own in one stunning location after another. When you sail into one of the small fishing towns that dot the coast, local children will paddle up to you in their traditional round basket boats, just to say hello. They have huge smiles. It's pretty apparent that they've never seen such a sailboat before, and that it's quite a spectacle."

Kevin Quilty is managing director of SunSail Thailand (www.sunsail.com), a post he's held since 1993. He oversees a fleet of over forty yachts, covering a cruising area that extends from Phuket to Langkawi, Malaysia, and also operates a Royal Yachting Association sailing school. Prior to coming to Thailand, Kevin served as a flotilla skipper for SunSail in Greece, Corsica, and Sardinia, and was assistant berthing manager at the Brighton Marina in the United Kingdom. He holds an RYA Ocean Yachtmaster Offshore certification, with instructor's endorsement.

▶ IF YOU GO ◀

➤ **Getting There:** Nha Trang is the point of departure for charters in Vietnam, and is a short flight from Ho Chi Minh City (Saigon). Flights to Ho Chi Minh City are available from San Francisco on Cathay Pacific, Delta, EVA, United, and Vietnam Airlines, among others.

➤ **Best Time to Visit:** The Nha Trang region has somewhat drier and more temperate weather than other regions of Vietnam. The available sailing season (per the government) is mid-May through mid-September.

➤ **Charter Operators:** At present, SunSail (888-350-3568; www.sunsail.com) is the only charter operator on the ground in Vietnam.

➤ **Moorings:** Modern sailboats are not often seen in these parts. There are few limitations upon where you can moor.

➤ **On-Shore Accommodations:** TraveltoVietnam.com (www.traveltovietnam.com) lists fifteen lodgings options in Nha Trang.

SAN JUAN ISLANDS

RECOMMENDED BY **Tim Mehrer**

Hundreds of thousands of tourists board ferries in Anacortes, Washington, and Victoria, British Columbia, each summer to take in the wonders of the San Juan Islands. Nearly as many cruisers join them. Fortunately, there's enough room for everyone!

"There are two beautiful aspects of the San Juans to me as a sailor," said Tim Mehrer. "First, it's simply gorgeous, especially on a clear day when the Olympics are visible to the west and Mount Baker and Mount Rainier to the east. Second, from a tactical perspective, you can always use the wind and current together to set a path. Because the islands are an archipelago, whether the tide is ebbing or flowing and wherever the wind is coming from, there's somewhere you can go to find a good anchorage. Sometimes a passenger will ask, 'Where are we going tonight?' My response is, 'Tell me where the wind is coming from, and then I'll tell you.' If you want heavier winds, you can head out into the Strait of Juan de Fuca. Pretty much everywhere else, you can find a beautiful cove and not have to worry about heavy water."

The San Juan Archipelago begins north of Puget Sound, roughly 60 miles north of Seattle, and stretches nearly 100 miles. Resting between Vancouver Island and the Strait of Juan de Fuca to the west, the Strait of Georgia to the north, and the mainland of Washington to the east, the islands were the historical home of the Salish people, who traveled from island to island in cedar canoes, subsisting primarily on salmon; indeed, the inland waters were once known as the Salish Sea. There are upward of seven hundred islands in the San Juan chain, though most of the area's residents live on the four largest islands—Orcas, San Juan, Lopez, and Shaw. (Some of the islands in the archipelago rest in Canadian territory and are called the Gulf Islands.) The San Juans are remnants of ancient mountain ranges that geologists believe were once part of a separate continent, one that predated North

America. Resting in the rain shadow of the Olympics, the islands have a much drier climate than the rest of western Washington. The buffering influence of Vancouver Island makes for generally tranquil conditions. All these factors combine to create a lush, temperate landscape with enough human settlement to make provisioning easy but enough isolation to give one exposure to a unique—and mostly intact—ecosystem.

A historical curiosity is that the San Juans were the site of one of the last territorial squabbles between Great Britain and the United States, and certainly one of the few near-wars inflamed by a pig. It seems that in 1859, said pig escaped from one Bellevue Farm (owned by Hudson's Bay) on several occasions to root about in the potato patch of an American settler named Lyman Cutlar. On seeing the pig approach, Cutlar dispatched the animal with his musketloader, and refused to compensate Bellevue Farm for its loss. Tensions escalated, underscoring the larger issue of territorial ownership, and both nations dispatched troops to the island. Ultimately, sovereignty was decided by Kaiser Wilhelm I, who was chosen to arbitrate the situation. He sided with the Americans, and the battle for the San Juans was settled without a human casualty.

A delight of cruising the San Juans is the variety the islands afford. "There's stuff to do for people of all skill and interest levels," Tim commented. "You can go wine tasting on Lopez Island at the Lopez Island Vineyards. Some like to check out the Hotel De Haro in upscale Roche Harbor, which is on the National Register of Historic Places, or go shopping in Friday Harbor. You can catch your dinner—salmon or crab, as many charter boats come equipped with crab pots. There are sandy beaches, rocky beaches, mountains to hike. Or you can find a quiet harbor and sit back and relax."

The variety afforded by the San Juans extends from activity to place. Friday Harbor, on the east side of San Juan Island, receives ferry passengers each day, yet has retained a funky flavor of its own despite being a tourist center. Roche Harbor, on the northwest tip of San Juan Island, is the place to rub elbows with blue-blooded sailors, some of whom moor their yachts in more tropical climes in the off-season. Suice Island, on the northeastern perimeter of the San Juans, is a favorite with cruisers, with ample anchorages and gunkholing opportunities. If you tire of the islands' more rural charms, Victoria, the capital city of British Columbia, is also within easy striking distance of the San Juans.

One of the great tourist draws of the San Juans is the chance to spy one of the orcas that call the islands home much of the year. Three pods—"J," "K," and "L"—make up eighty-five to ninety killer whales, and are generally known as the Southern Resident

OPPOSITE
Though it's easy to find solitude in the San Juans, services are never far away.

DESTINATION

49

Community. (Researchers and amateur whale enthusiasts can identify each animal by the shape of its dorsal fin and its "saddle patch," the gray markings associated with orcas.) "There was a time when you would hear the orcas breathing before you saw them," Tim recalled. "Now, you look for the orange boats of whale-tour operators! Seriously, though, the best time to see orcas is when we're under sail and all the whale-watching boats are off the water—generally earlier or later in the day. We also encounter Dall's porpoise, pygmy porpoise, sometime a minke whale, and always thousands of seals.

Tim Mehrer has been sailing the schooner *Zodiac* since 1975 and has been leading guests on chartered tours around the San Juan Islands and British Columbia since 1988. Built in 1924, the *Zodiac* (www.schoonerzodiac.com) is the largest operating sailing ship on the West Coast of the United States. Tim gained his passion for wooden boats from his dad, who did a great deal of boat restoration. Before sailing the *Zodiac* as a vocation, Tim and his father ran an industrial boiler business. Three generations of Mehrers—Tim, his dad, and his son—work on the *Zodiac* in the summer months.

IF YOU GO

➤ **Getting There:** Anacortes, Washington—about ninety miles north of Seattle—is a common point of departure for the San Juans. Ferry service (www.wsdot.wa.gov/ferries) is available from Anacortes, as is plane service (www.sanjuanairlines.com).

➤ **Best Time to Visit:** The San Juans have a cool but pleasant climate. The most pleasant conditions will be encountered from mid-spring to mid-fall.

➤ **Charter Operators:** Bareboats are available from Anacortes through ABC Yacht Charters (800-426-2313; www.abcyachtcharters.com) and from Friday Harbor through Charters Northwest (800-258-3119; www.chartnersnorthwest.com).

➤ **Moorings:** Marina services are available on San Juan, Lopez and Orcas Islands. The Port of Friday Harbor (360-378-2688; www.portfridayharbor.org/marina) has many slips available for transient sailors.

➤ **On-Shore Accommodations:** The San Juan Islands Visitors Bureau (888-468-3701; www.guidetosanjuans.com) provides a list of lodgings options on the San Juans.

ST. VINCENT AND
THE GRENADINES

RECOMMENDED BY **Steve Mason**

The producers of *Pirates of the Caribbean* could have chosen just about anywhere in the Caribbean—or the world, for that matter—to film their blockbuster. That they chose St. Vincent and the Grenadines speaks to the island's picture-perfect representation of the Caribbean's allure.

"St. Vincent and the Grenadines have things to offer that you don't find in other regions of the Caribbean," Steve Mason began. "First, the islands are clustered fairly close together, but not *too* close together. You can have a nice day sail from one anchorage to another, but not *too much* of a day sail—you can still anchor with plenty of daylight, and have time to take the kids snorkeling. When you leave an anchorage, you can't see your next destination. You just have your chart and headings. But you still get there the same day. Eventually you'll see something in the distance, and three hours later, you're there. Second, the islands lie north to south, so all of your sails are nice even tacks. Third, you get very strong winds coming in off the Atlantic; as you move further west in the Caribbean, the winds are not as consistent. Around the Windward Islands, sailing can get quite adventurous—you can test your skills both as a family man and as a man. It's a little less traveled than other parts of the Caribbean, probably because it's a little tougher to sail."

The Windward Islands rest at the eastern edge of the Caribbean. They take their name from the fact that they were more *windward* for ships arriving from Europe and other points east than their counterparts to the west, the Leeward Islands. The Windward chain includes Martinique, St. Lucia, Barbados, St. Vincent, The Grenadines, Grenada, Trinidad, and Tobago. The northern islands, from Martinique to St. Vincent, are volcanic, with peaks eclipsing 3,000 feet and with rugged coastlines. (Soufrière on St. Vincent is over 4,000 feet tall and is still active, erupting as recently at 1979.) The six hundred small islands

of the Grenadines have a gentler aspect, with broad, white sand beaches, often sheltered by coral reefs. St. Vincent is roughly 200 miles north of the coastline of Venezuela.

Like many West Indian islands, St. Vincent and the Grenadines were settled by Europeans, who quickly dispensed of the Caribs native to the area and established sugar plantations by the mid-1700s. Many black African slaves were brought here to work the cane fields; most of the islands' residents are descendants of slaves. The plantations thrived until the early nineteenth century, when Europeans discovered that sugar beets, which could be grown at home, could sate their collective sugar tooth. Demand for cane declined, and residents of the islands returned to subsistence agriculture and fishing. Agriculture is still important, with bananas being the chief cash crop. Tourism has become increasingly important to the nation's economy in the last thirty years. Since 1979, St. Vincent and the Grenadines has been an independent nation, part of the British Commonwealth.

St. Vincent is generally the point of departure for bareboat sailors, and most will head south. (It's worth nothing that the mountains and rainforest of interior St. Vincent are worthy of exploration in themselves!) For Steve, one of the first ports of call might be the island of Bequia, the second-largest island in the Grenadines. Bequia includes an active tourist spot, Port Elizabeth, which is on Admiralty Bay, the island's main port. There are also the requisite secluded, clean, and uncrowded beaches. One point of interest that Steve took in was the Old Hegg Turtle Sanctuary. "It's just a few miles north of Port Elizabeth. The founder—Brother King—is trying to reestablish the native turtle population. This guy has found that mortality is greatest in the first few years of their lives, so he collects eggs or catches the turtles when they're born, and protects and feeds them." According to his Web site, Brother King has over 250 hawksbill turtles that he will eventually release into the wild.

The next stop south for Steve might be Mustique. "It's a private island, inhabited by extremely rich people who live in massive homes. It was once a British settlement, and still has a distinctly British flavor." A center of sugar plantations in the early nineteenth century, Mustique went into decline with the introduction of sugar beets in Europe, which dried up demand for cane. Its revitalization began in 1958 with its purchase by a Scottish lord, the Honorable Colin Tennant. Tennant helped reinvigorate the agricultural activities on the island, and ushered in the notion of high-end tourism development. The resulting community has included such part-time residents as Mick Jagger, David Bowie, and Princess Margaret of England. "There's a great bar in Brittania Bay [Mustique's main

OPPOSITE
When the
producers of
Pirates of the
Caribbean
wanted a
picture-perfect
seascape,
they chose the
Grenadines.

DESTINATION

50

harbor] called Basil's that's worth a visit," Steve said. "We also like to stop in at the Cottonhouse, a very high-end resort." Mustique in general is high-end; some rental homes during the winter are available for as much as $30,000 a week.

Another favorite stop in the Grenadines is Tobago Keys, a bit farther down the island string, near Grenada. "It's a series of four small islands—Petit Rameau, Barabel, Petit Bateau, and Jamesby. Beyond the reef, there's nothing but the Atlantic. The beaches are incredibly pristine. We had some amazing snorkeling there, some of the best I've experienced anywhere." The Tobago Keys have been set aside as a nature refuge, which has enabled them to maintain their Caribbean-paradise aura. "There's no development to speak of on the Tobago Keys," Steve continued. "But there are skiffs that will come out and sell you ice, beer, rum, fresh fish, etc. It's great—you're in the middle of nowhere, but there's this little service to deliver you all the amenities you could want."

For Steve and his family, it's become a small tradition—whenever possible—to spend the Christmas holidays floating off the Windward Islands. "By the time we get to December, there's a sentiment of 'NO MORE CHRISTMAS' in our house. So we try to get to the Windwards. We'll bring some vestiges of the holiday along—hang our stockings somewhere on the boat, and open some gifts. While we have those elements of Christmas with us, the last thought on our mind is of snow and winter."

Steve Mason is a photographer based in Olympia, Washington (www.masonimage.com). Over the past twenty years he has built a reputation for delivering high-quality images for his clients. Steve is an accomplished sailor, skier, climber, surfer, and all-around outdoorsman who has blended these unique skills with his training, experience, and finesse to produce dynamic work. Known to rappel from cliffs in the German Alps, skipper a bareboat yacht in the Caribbean, or slog through the *sawahs* (rice patties) of Southeast Asia, he has the proven ability to get to these rugged, exotic locales, and the seamlessness and subtlety required to deliver the shot. Steve's extensive client list includes Eddie Bauer, L. L. Bean, Nordstrom's, Wrangler, REI, JCPenney, Early Winters, Home Depot, and Holland America, to list just a few. In addition, Steve has done work with Flying Doctors of America in Venezuela and sailed in Force 9 conditions into Havana harbor aboard a three-masted schooner. He spends his free time with his wife of twenty-four years and their two children—sailing their 43-foot *Hans Christian* out of Olympia, skiing, and being fully immersed in each other.

IF YOU GO

➤ **Getting There:** Most will start their travels on St. Vincent; some will depart from St. Vincent as well. Others may choose to sail one way to Union or Grenada. St. Vincent is served (with flights connecting from Barbados, Puerto Rico, St. Lucia, Martinique, and Grenada) by many carriers, including American, Delta, United, and U.S. Airways.

➤ **Best Time to Visit:** Though winds and weather are fairly constant (and wonderful) throughout the year, the winter months are the most popular time to visit.

➤ **Charter Operators:** A number of companies operate among these popular cruising grounds. Windward Islands (954-873-2003; www.caribbean-adventure.com) and SunSail (888-350-3568; www.sunsail.com) both offer bareboat charters from the southern tip of St. Vincent.

➤ **Moorings:** Anchorages are plentiful as you make your way south from St. Vincent.

➤ **On-Shore Accommodations:** The St. Vincent and the Grenadines Ministry of Tourism and Culture (www.svgtourism.com) lists available accommodations on the islands that offer lodgings.

Published in 2007 by Stewart, Tabori & Chang
An imprint of Harry N. Abrams, Inc.

Library of Congress Cataloging-in-Publication Data
Santella, Chris.
Fifty places to sail before you die : sailing experts share the world's
greatest destinations / Chris Santella.
p. cm.
ISBN-13: 978-1-58479-567-4
ISBN-10: 1-58479-567-0
1. Sailing—Guidebooks. 2. Sailing—Directories. I. Title.
GV811.S264 2007
797.124—dc22
2006031881

Editor: Jennifer Levesque
Production Manager: Jacquie Poirier
Book design: Paul Wagner

The text of this book was composed in Interstate, Ionic,
and News Plantin typefaces.

Photograph credits:
Pages 2, 10, 12, 76, 92, 108, 122, 130, 140, 144, 162,180: © Billy Black/www.billyblack.com; Pages 16, 38, 48, 68,
72, 80, 134, 216, 220: © Bob Grieser/OutsideImages.co.nz; Page 20: © Skip Novak; Page 26: © Th. Martinez;
Page 30: © Kos Picture Source, Ltd.; Page 34: © Tourism New South Wales; Page 54: © John Neal; Page 84: ©
Gilles Martin-Raget; Page 88: © Amanda Swan Neal; Page 96: © 2006 Phil Uhl; Page 100: © Karen I. Hirsch/www.
kihphoto.com; Page 104: © Carlo Borlenghi/Rolex; Page 112: © Benjamin Mendlowitz; Page 126: © Tally Garfield;
Pages 148, 170, 204: © Onne van der Wal/www.vanderwal.com; Page 154: © Nova Scotia Tourism, Culture and
Heritage; Pages 158, 194: © Sharon Matthews-Stevens; Page 174: © Sailactive Private Yachting; Page 184: ©
Kevin Swigert/Warbonnet Entertainment; Page 190: © Susan Maffei Plowden; Page 198: © Isle of Wight Tourism/
www.islandbreaks.co.uk

Page 2: Off Newport, Rhode Island, you'll encounter everything from
America's Cup racers to turn-of-the century wooden boats.

Printed and bound in China
10 9 8 7 6 5 4 3 2 1

HNA
harry n. abrams, inc.
a subsidiary of La Martinière Groupe
115 West 18th Street
New York, NY 10011
www.hnabooks.com